Gifts of H

Lynette

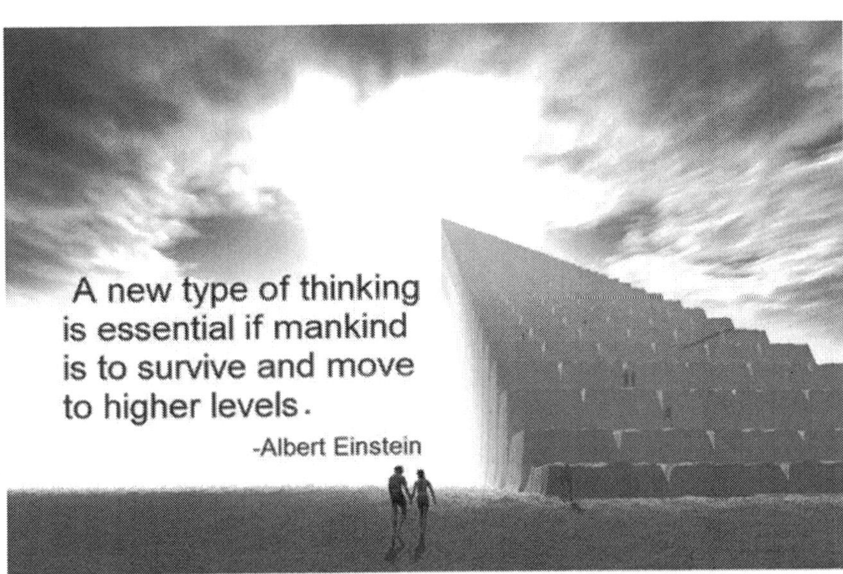

This book presents simple logical that is a way to relate to our imagination and emotions that surpass the challenges of a modern world. We can reach greater heights of potential than ever before.

Lynette R. Wyatt LVN III/RCFE Admin.

Health and Wellness Director/RCFE Admin.

Lynette has for 30 years worked with centennials, and is amazed by the stories of their lives. What better way is there to learn about our humanity than from those who lived to enjoy a long and successful life? What drove them through their hardships, what brought them solace, and what kept their faith and hopes bright? What virtues and habits did they have in common? She found that they answered their challenges and prospered because of their common gifts of humanity that anyone of us could develop. Lynette's insights into our humanity provide us the solutions.

Forward

A species is defined by the unique attributes that help it to thrive and enjoy a full life. Like with a dog's keen sense of smell, allowing it to hunt, survive, and have an abundant life. Our unique gifts also define our humanity and bring us a fullness of life. But unlike other species that do so by instincts, our gifts are developed by choice, hard work, and time.

Many of our hopes are universal, such as happiness, great relationships, successful careers, and peaceful societies. Together we can make these dreams a reality by helping each other in the course of reaching our potential. Our shared hopes cannot be attained except for by developing our humanity. Our gifts answer our challenges and help us cope through life. These gifts are changeless. They have the power to evolve us to unimaginable heights.

Steven R Covey said, “People can't live with change if there's not a changeless core inside them. The key to the ability to change is a changeless sense of who you are, what you are about, and what you value”.

Knowing what our innate gifts are is not enough. We also need to know the virtues and truths which guide our gifts for our well-being. We need core beliefs that don't change as we struggle for understanding. We need beliefs that relate to our potential and that put things into perspective. We need beliefs that don't change with recent trends but transcend culture and disrobe falsehoods. We do not need psychology textbooks that are outmoded by the time they are printed. This is our time to live, we need to get it right, and we deserve to know the truth!

Table of Contents

Section 1
Blueprints of Humanity

These first four chapters define our humanity, for everything that we build we first create spiritually. All things are first born of our imaginations. That is, we make blueprints, draw up plans, and consider all the possible obstacles. We first consider all the things that we will need. For example, if we want our custom made home we must first imagine what it will look like. How big will it be, and what will it be made of? What is the nature of our humanity? What is its full potential? How will we achieve it? In this section, we will make blueprints in a language of words we have well defined, and discuss them in a way we all can understand and build from.

Chapter 1- Humanity Defined

The wind has shifted, I will not falter
As waves crash upon the bow, I look on
Be steady my faith, and patient my soul
Till my vessel reaches the harbor's shore

Section 1
Humanity defined

When we are awed by the sun setting on the bay, or we are surprised by our toddlers taking their first steps, we are witnessing life's magnificence. Nature is beautiful and inspiring. Perhaps, even with all the amazing things, we witness in this world, nature's crowning achievement is humanity- mainly because nature's gift to us allows us to do some creating of our own.

One microscopic strand of DNA enables us to imagine, play, smile, laugh, invent, paint, tell stories, dream, sing, play musical instruments... and this list goes on ad infinitum. Nature's gifts to us is an endless litany of possibilities. For example, the culmination of nature's gifts to mankind allows us to read books containing the shared imagination and knowledge of those who lived long ago. This ability to learn perhaps is the most helpful gift for humanity. We can expand upon the efforts of those who preceded us. We can create more loving families, healthier lifestyles, and even further explore the cosmos.

"The beginning of wisdom is the definition of terms."
-Socrates

Defining agency, freedom, soul, and humanity

Our humanity is human attributes or qualities that not only we can have as a race, but that we all can develop in an abundance. And the soul is the total embodiment of all an individual possesses, in the body and in mind, with which life is experienced. Our soul then enjoys the most complete and deepest experiences with our world.

Agency is the faculty that acts on behalf of one's self, and freedom is the right and depths of our opportunity to use our agency. In courts, we call agency the power of attorney. We have that right to act in our own behalf or we can share that right with an attorney to act for us.

Our agency is always in play, and regardless of many forced obstructions placed on us, usually by governing powers, we can still choose what thoughts we have and what character we will develop. But, as for now, our freedom is constantly being fought for from one generation to another. If we are stuck in philosophical debates of whether or not humans "should" live free, then humanity is stuck at the docking port; when, we could be using our agency to freely sail to and find exotic lands. For us to rise to a higher level of humanity the battle for our individual freedom must be resolved and our efforts focused on self-reliance and harmonious living.

The dual nature of our humanity

The gifts of our humanity are like a magic lamp, and at the same time, they are also a Pandora's Box. For our agency has the power to choose and build incredible things and at the same time, it has the power to do great harm. For with the power to create also comes the power to destroy, this is the risk nature took in giving us its greatest gifts. The paradox is nature and our humanity can be destroyed by the very gifts we were given. These powerful gifts are in the hands of humanity's adolescent purview.

A study of such dual nature is from the University of Nebraska in October-2011 "Cantankerous creativity Honesty-Humility, Agreeableness, and the HEXACO structure of creative achievement," by Paul Silvia, James Kaufman, Roni ReiterPalmon, and Benjamin Wigert. This study brings to light creative people tell lies more often than those who are not as creative. We might conclude being honest, as a creative person, takes more effort. The positive side of creativity is that we can be more tactful when sharing information that is hard to hear. With creativity, we find more possible answers and achieve more success.

This dual nature is a choice for us, neither is forced upon us, but whether we use these gifts for the good or evil is up to us. We are the captains of our souls and we decide what direction to sail the ship we call our soul. It is captained by our agency and its sails are our imagination and beliefs. We can sail through life reacting to adverse winds, or we can sail against the winds of opposition to a determined port.

In our voyage in life, we will find that the Sirens that hold us catatonic are those of our own lust and greed. The serpents that poison us are our own pride and selfishness. And the sorceresses that distort our reality are our own fears and superstitions. The success of our journey depends on our determination to overcome weakness and challenge. We must keep sailing more effectively and more accurately until we reach a halcyon port.

The gifts that define us are those we hold in abundance

Not all the gifts defining us are unique to ourselves. What makes them the defining gifts of our humanity is that these are the gifts in which we have, or in which we can develop, in an abundance. It is the same with other species. The eagle has eyes allowing it to see a rodent a mile away. It is in the abundance of particular abilities that the eagle has that prospers it.

Humanity's unique set of gifts allows us to prosper in unimaginable ways.

All of us were born meant to become great. Nobody is born meant to be a slave. Nobody is born meant to remain uneducated. Nobody belongs to or should be stuck in any caste in society. We were not born to be anything in particular. We were born to be anything we would ever want to be. This is our heritage.

The higher and nobler path is always a possible choice

Except for humanity, the potential for living things is achieved by biological compulsion. What an animal or a plant becomes is stringently predestined. An apple seed matures into a tree bearing its own particular fruit. It is defined by the fruit it bears. With our humanity, we must "choose" to develop the gifts nascent within us. This is a tremendous task worth every effort. We are not "predestined" to be anything; we always have a choice. But the dual nature of our gifts implies that we do have an ideal direction to choose and traverse.

Unlike the instinct of animals, our agency can choose paths that lead away from human potential. This is because our agency always has the final say in my "choices," not my appetites, or my moods and feelings, not even my genetic inclinations. Agency usually, by default and in half-baked efforts, finds itself on errant paths- unless it proactively and in relevant ways, choosing its course even in the worst of times. In fact, choosing well in hard times is a must if we are going to be what nature implied for us in our gifts.

The importance of knowing "Who we are"

For clarity in this book, "who we are" is the seeds that germinate and ripen into our potential. That we, like all life, just developed the fruit we were meant to. We simply chose to pursue and develop the better of the two paths, to develop our gifts. "Who we are" represents the ripe fruit we were meant to bear as if we had chosen to develop the gifts of our humanity. We are predetermined for greatness, because of the unfathomable gifts we were given. (See figure 1 at the end of section four in this chapter.)

Unlike the flora around us, using 100 percent of its potential, we spend our time only using a fraction of our potential. To exacerbate our efforts in life, we spend a great amount of time developing vices and hardly notice it. Though we see exactly what an apple tree is meant to be, the seeds of our humanity are not so apparent. We only get a small glimpse of all we can be.

If we were to stand next to our potential self, it would transform our lives. We would do unimaginably incredible things. Studying human behavior and human possibilities, by studying animals, is like studying jet planes by watching leaves blown in the wind. When humans "fly" we do so in spite of the wind and the gravity of our circumstance.

Once we know what our possibilities are we would do whatever it takes to attain them. These possibilities include every soul born within the human race, from those born with autism or down-syndrome to those who are considered prodigies. Every soul, which comes to an understanding of all they could be, would set themselves on a course more firmly headed for greatness.

Knowing what we are capable of puts our feet on a secure path

Knowing who we are is an anchor for self-identity, and it is the lodestar for which a steady course is set. It is also the impetus by which we weather the storm. Actually seeing an amazingly intelligent, articulate, and successful future me- helps me to understand that I am not stupid, just unschooled. I am not broken, there is just more assembly is required.

Like the small lion cub who sees his father as strong, large, and capable. A cub understands this is what it is meant to be.

When I left for school my mother said, "Remember who you are!" She reminded me of the principles she taught me, and that I should live by what I knew to be right. She reminded me of the great things I could accomplish if I walked my own course and didn't just go with the crowd. She also sarcastically said when I acted up, "Just who do you think you are!" Implying that I am definitely not who I should be. Teaching me to remember who I really am is how she kept me grounded. It was my standard. It was a reminder to me to remember my worth.

The instilling of who I am, from a wise mother, taught me what true greatness was. It isn't about popularity or being cool. It was to live by my own conscience, respect for myself, and a respect for others. It was about being an honest and genuine human being, a person that doesn't cower or feel shame about being myself.

We enjoy being with those people who are true to who they are

One thing you learn, when working with the elderly for so many years, is that we are not identified by our profession, hobbies, the roles we play, the college degrees we hold, or the awards we win. This is especially more apparent as we come to the end of our lives. These are not who we are. These are some of the things we do and accomplish with who we are. These are the things we do with our gifts. We accomplish our unique goals, and reach our personal dreams, with those gifts we all have in common waiting to be developed.)

A single accomplishment, a college degree, a horrific mistake, or a bad choice isn't who we are. Identifying ourselves from our professions, hobbies, and accomplishments hinder our efforts in being true to who we really are. These epithets, used as identities to esteem, slow or dam our progress in those things that matter most.

If you were living on a deserted island and had only one person to share it with, would you choose an honest and caring person with no titles or accomplishments to boast of? Or, would you share it with a rocket scientist or an Olympic medalist who is dishonest and selfish? (What is it then that makes an admirable human being?)

Section 2
Truth and its relevance to our humanity

Agency and personal accountability for our gifts

This is not a book about positive thinking, self-assertiveness, or self-esteem. This book is not a "do whatever you want to do book," as if our choices do not affect others or end on paths without regrets. This is not a book that will tell us things we want to hear and that sound good. This is not a book with simple magic formulas for success. This book is frank. It will tell the tough truths many will not want to hear. It "will" question things most of us believe in.

Maritime captains do not crew their ships on perilous journeys with positive thinking farmers. They do not fill it with yeomen that did whatever they wanted to do, just because it sounded good at the time. They fill their crew with those knowledgeable, skilled, and faithful at their duties.

The path to our potential is also the path of truth. We are the only species that can believe in truth, and conversely, we are the only species can believe in lies. When we believe in the fiction within our souls, we will make our choices on the assumption these lies will take us to where we want to go. Regardless of the social acceptance of the lie, how beautiful a lie may seem, and how titillating its deception is- no amount of positive thinking, that captains behind a lie, will work for our happiness. Positive thinking, self-assertiveness, and self-esteem will fall short; because they do not focus on gaining pertinent knowledge and skills directed toward our potential.

Humanity is fighting a war of truths and falsehoods

Humanity's biggest war is not fought with guns but with truths and falsehoods. It is a battle for our "freedom," for our agency to have more possibilities and dreams to choose from. It seems a common thread throughout history. Its factions are often unknowingly carrying out the battle. In the end, only the truth can bring peace and happiness.

Our quandary is that truth doesn't come with a truth label, nor is it always fashionable and easy. But ugly truths will make beautiful human beings and fulfilling relationships, and existential and beautiful sounding lies make for contentions and misunderstandings.

We have to see past the popular beliefs and find the relevant truths to who we are. If we can't think beyond the beliefs that are in consensus in our culture, then we cannot think critically or logically. Each must learn to think for one's self. In the next chapters, we will discuss how to determine what is true.

An enormous challenge of our humanity is that it can be very difficult to distinguish fact from fiction. Those that would profit from deceiving us have great sounding lies and seemingly altruistic reasons. In the end, erroneous beliefs are a divergence from the joy we could have known from being free, capable, and self-reliant human beings.

True freedom is gained by the individual who is honest and open enough to find the truth, and fearless enough to live by it.

Section 3
Technology and humanity

The arrival of technology and invention has created a dilemma for humanity. Since 1830 AD every five years information has doubled. Taking all the knowledge that humanity has amassed before 1830 as one unit, we now have 1.95 trillion times more information than just 188 years ago.

Invention facilitates life. Today we have a course that allows us to be far lazier than we have been through human history and still "survive." Because our load is light, we have become weak. With this weakness, we have become a generation that exaggerates the weight of their problems. And since physical and emotional pain shares the same neurons in the brain, our emotional pain feels all too real. With this increasing emotional pain, we are ever more seeking drugs to anesthetize it.

Technology has taken away a lot of life's natural opposition that builds emotional strength

The average age to cope with adult problems in 1945 was 16 years old. Today, emotional maturity isn't reached on average until after 40 years of age. That is because more than fifty percent of Americans still worked on farms before 1935. Those leaving the farms after 1935, still had the work ethic from a hard life. They pushed themselves to succeed. See book "Emotional Intelligence" by Daniel Goldman.

This book devotes two chapters to emotions, because of the growing disparity between advancing technology and regressing emotional maturity. Our dilemma is so pressing that the next generation is not likely to reach an age where they will be able to cope with their problems. As life becomes easier they are less able to cope with adult problems, and everyday situations needing a mature individual causes them deep emotional pain.

An awakening is needed about our humanity, the way we see ourselves and the way we choose to find satisfaction in life. We need an awakening that causes us to more fully push ourselves, rather than life pushing us, with the specific purpose in becoming complete individuals. We need an understanding permeating our world about our self-worth, our capabilities, and the relevant efforts that are absolutely necessary for our happiness.

The generation in 1945, that push themselves to work hard, was replaced by succeeding generations growing lazier in proportion to our expanding technology. Each generation now is more prone to instant and constant gratification, and to new minimal efforts for survival. They escape the challenges we need for developing our gifts but not the consequences. There is a silver lining to this. If we learn to push ourselves, to grow in character and develop our gifts, then we can evolve far more than we could without technology.

The growing need for greater efforts and purer motives because of technology's power to facilitate human activity

Technology is an extension of human power or a replacement of human power. We are creating things to extend our reach, sight, mobility, and the computing power of our minds. We are extending the sensitivities and abilities of the human soul. We are seeing farther with a telescope, traveling faster with a jet, and higher with a rocket. We are connecting to people anywhere at any time.

It isn't just the inventions of high tech devices that are making our lives easy. It is true in medicine as well. This impediment to our gifts is more to blame on our agency than it is on technology. We are not motivating ourselves to creatively find ways to develop our virtues and skills.

Working hard on virtues and skills makes life easier while working easily on skills and virtues makes our lives harder. Working hard in all the right ways makes life an incredible journey.

Our efforts to marginally get through life without developing a hard work ethic or gaining emotional fortitude makes us weak in all areas of our lives. This even includes our efforts to think rationally. We exacerbate the problem when we try to make life easy for our children. They do not associate hard work with getting things. They are unable to make a sufficient effort to have the skills to achieve what they want when they are finally on their own.

Inventions in medicine are now being used as our most destructive crutch. We need to stop believing life shouldn't be hard and stop fearing to make the necessary exceptional effort. Simple tasks, that were easy for those that worked hard a generation ago, are hard for those of us who are now used to just getting by. When we grow in coping skills and work ethic, our challenges are still hard but we are stronger to succeed regardless of them.

We can start with simple tasks like going to sleep without the aid of a sleeping pill, becoming alert without a stimulant, being able to calm and relax without the help of alcohol. We do not need a pill for our mercurial emotions, or for our attention deficiency. We can gain the confidence and ability to do things with our own inner power.

Section 4
Our gifts are sufficient for potential and happiness

We need a new way of thinking around our difficult emotions

The common gifts of our humanity are the most powerful force for human achievement, and our agency always has the final say to choose our gifts.

In our sailing through life, we can study all the winds that blow and the direction the wind blows. Some would do anything to keep the winds from blowing. It seems that the new norm is to make every effort to stop feeling the adversarial winds blowing. Unfortunately feeling the wind blowing and its direction is needed information for the care of our humanity. How strong our discordant emotions show us how irrational, how weak, and unprepared we are.

In our modern world, we need to be even more quickly aware and emotionally adept than ever before, not less so. We need to be even more proactive in each stage in life to prepare for the next stage. We need to be taught what these emotions mean and how to answer their reasons for being. We need to stop blaming others for how unhappy we are and take personal responsibility for it.

Albert Einstein said, "A new type of thinking is essential if mankind is to survive and move to higher levels." This book presents that this new way of thinking, and understanding our emotions, is answered best by using the gifts of our humanity as criteria for respect, love, and truth. They are represented by the North Star figure illustrated at the end of this section of this chapter, representing our gifts in embryo.

Instead of a growing number of perceived psychosis and half our children on drugs we can reverse the insanity. We can teach our children a new way of thinking about their emotions instead of fearing them. We can teach them how to read and respond to their emotions in ways that build a strong sense of worth; a self-motivation that is without prejudice, arrogance, or fear.

Our agency gives life more meaning

When our agency took the helm of our humanity it made for a far deeper and more meaningful experience with life. Having to choose those things that are true to "who we are" makes life more meaningful. How loving would it be to do something kind, if it were instinctual? How much could we appreciate a sunset, if appreciation were instinctual? If we were honest by instinct, we would be robots and couldn't lie when it kept us safe. How exciting would it be to win an athletic event, if it were not earned by our own determination and hard work? How considerate could we be, if we had never been disrespected, hurt, or sick? Our flaws can make us beautiful. They can make us tender, compassionate, wise, and give us purpose.

It does not matter what unique predispositions an individual might have that are inherent from birth. Our agency and the gifts we have in common stand towering above them. This is the force that really matters. We answer all our problems with our human potential. Even if that answer, at least to start with, is to simply learn to be happy in our lives despite our depression or a physical handicaps. We will discuss how in later chapters.

As long as we can imagine a better world, our agency can learn and choose new pathways to brighter futures.

Developed skills and virtues trump I.Q. and natural talent

Each one of us, with our agency and with the proper use of our gifts, can reach our ultimate human potential. Even those born with high I.Q. will be surpassed in intelligence by those who develop their human faculties. Faculties are those abilities for which we all can develop or have in common. The height of our intelligence results from the proper use of our agency, not the intellectual quotient we were born with.

We all can be extremely intelligent when we develop the gifts we have in common. I.Q. is an insignificant factor in our overall intellect. It is an insignificant factor in our effectiveness in pursuing our dreams, and in making a difference in the lives of those around us. In modern times, no employers are hiring employees because of their high I.Q.

We used to believe I.Q. was innate, but we have learned it can be developed by exercising our faculties. (See article from Earl Hunt Ph.D. "Improving Intelligence"). We can calculate in our minds the total of the groceries before they are fully checked out. We can discriminate the different flavors and textures in the food we eat. We can get a sense of which direction north is before we look at the G.P.S. We can exercise the gifts of humanity.

We are neither better than others because of a special genetic inheritance, the "prodigy," nor are we disadvantaged because of the lack of any such outstanding gifts in the course of our lives. Our common gifts of humanity, in which we all need to develop, will eventually be triumphant over the challenges that are set before us. In the end, the race will go to the one who developed their common gifts of humanity, not to the one who had a few easy steps at first because of genetic serendipity.

The gifts of our humanity include our ability to gain knowledge, be objective, be creative, and use our imaginations for our well-being. Our gifts include developing virtues, adhering to principles, and developing skills. A skill is an adept use of a human faculty for our benefit. Some of the skills that we can develop our critical thinking skills, work skills, language skills, listening skills, and emotional skills. Virtues are principles of admirable conduct that have become a part of our character. Some of the gifts of our humanity include virtues like honesty and humility, causing us to be more teachable, and empathy, bringing compassion that rectifies our insensitive choices, apologizes for and restores what was taken. All of which keeps us from rationalizing false beliefs and ugly vices.

How adept one may be at a skill, nobody knows, how deeply strong, and ingrained a virtue can be, nobody can tell. Throughout the book, the North Star will represent the main categories of our unique gifts of humanity. It represents "who we are."

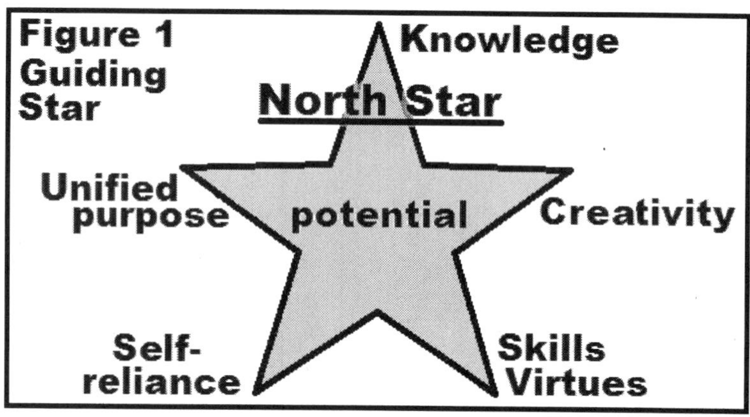

Section 5

Justice the enforcement of respect for our humanity

Rights are the boundaries respected surrounding the gifts of our humanity

Rights are defined by the boundaries of respect. Think of the star as the effort to 1) evolve ourselves as well as 2) the efforts needed to hold ourselves in worth and to protect ourselves. These boundaries of where I begin and end are defined by the common attributes of humanity. Our rights simply mean that we do not need permission to use our gifts of humanity.

A right is:
A) Our freedom to choose to develop and use our own human faculties and skills without restrictions, or without a need for permission from anyone, including from any political or social bodies.
B) Our freedom to have ownership, choice, and self-protection over our own bodies, and over the things for which we have created or earned. Such creation and unified purpose include the family unit. It needs to be autonomous as long as it does not interfere with the individual boundaries of each member.
C) Our freedom to not be forced to be dependent on others, or other societal constructs such as government.
D) Our freedom to assemble with "mutual purpose"; such as religious gatherings, company meetings, celebratory gatherings, reunions, political affiliations, civil purposes, and so on.

Boundaries are:
A natural consequence of building virtues from the motive of respect, such as honesty, empathy, and respect. True boundaries within us are character traits. We are born with some innate enmity against evil, lewdness, irreverent behavior, etc. With a healthy childhood, free from chaos, boundaries come more naturally. Once torn down in the poor use of our agency/imagination they are difficult to rebuild. See Ch.8, Sec.6

"Building the boundaries that keep depression away"

Within these defining criteria "Our North Star", rights are not entitlements to things or conditions that can be created by our gifts. In other words, we have the right to use our gifts to obtain our desires but not the "right" to have the usury of someone else's gifts to get what we want or even what we need. Our rights end where someone else's rights begin. Each one of us chooses what gifts they will develop and what dreams they will pursue.

Justice is an effort to defend and ensure equal individual rights. With them, we reach our potential and achieve our individual dreams. As an individual, who cares for all people, I hope that this freedom, and subsequent justice, will finally prevail in my country and spread to all nations. With the assisted living residents, in the communities I have worked with, I have spoken to many servicemen and women who sacrificed years of their lives. They fought for their nation's freedoms as well as for the freedoms of other nations. I may not need to be as brave as putting my life in jeopardy, but I do hope I can be a part of spreading freedom throughout the world. I fight against the ignorance of who we are and oppression that would hold us back.

Chapter 2- Truth Defined

The sun is setting
And the ship is gently swaying.
The stagnant air and sullen fog
Haunt the timid crew.
The loadstars light that would guide them
Cannot be found in the sextant view.

Section 1
Truth is the path and the light for the path

Anciently sailors navigated by using the North Star to take the ship's bearings. It was also called the Lodestar. They did this because the North Star is always in the same place in the night's sky. As a reference point, the North Star helped them steer the ship in the right direction.

Our agency needs fundamental truths, so obviously true, that we know we can chart our course from them. These truths are the embodiment of "who we are". These truths are our North Star to guide humanity. Figure 1 is a rough model of these truths. The individual thinker grasps principles of freedom, happiness, success, and human potential... they are fundamentally related and they are his or her standard to judge contemporary beliefs and temporary solutions. They are the standard to judge what is real and has true cause and effect in our lives.

As I work with residents who have increasing dementia their level of care rises- for, as they lose grips on reality, they need further assistance living their lives. Their freedoms are restricted as the gifts of their gifts of humanity wither.

Truth doesn't do its work and then watch by the sidelines. It is not a spectator. Truth is the path upon which life progresses. Truths are needed to make our goals a reality. Our knowledge of truth lights up the path, whether this path is to reach Mars with a rocket or craft a government that frees and prospers society. Adherence to principles of truth is needed in every roll we play- like a father, husband, homemaker, mother, or wife. This adherence is needed in every pursuit we choose- such as an artist, doctor, athlete, banker, actor, or even an independent person.

Truth is verified by more than just cause and effect toward our goals. It is felt and seen in the unity and joy we have with those we share our world. The more truths we live together, the more unity we will then enjoy as friends and couples.

Without a clear definition of words, coming to a clear understanding of truth couldn't be reached. Without a clear definition of keywords, an understanding of the truth could not be spread throughout a society. Unlike many books that start spewing facts that can be explained in so many ways and scientific books that will be outmoded in less than a decade, this book defines things that do not change- realities such as what a human is and what virtues are.

Section 2
The capacity of our minds

Our capacity for storing knowledge and building upon truths

We have a near unlimited capacity to store knowledge. In our brains, we have the computing power that far exceeds any supercomputers today. We have the hardware of our minds which can hold 2.5 thousand terabytes of information. "Robert A Freitas, "The Future of Computers", _Analog_, March 1996." This is equivalent to leaving the TV on for 300 years or retaining the information of 5 billion books. There is enough, and to spare, when it comes to the hardware which we call our brains.

When it comes to the software in our minds, there are no limitations to what we can create

Invention and creativity is the organization of facts into new combinations. We can only combine two facts to create one combination. But with ten facts we can create one thousand and thirteen different combinations. The number of things we can create grow exponentially with increasing information.

With 2.5 thousand terabytes of information what we can invent, create, and solve is a number so large as to be incomprehensible.

Even with the billions that live on this planet, each one of us could write unique songs, invent new things, hold unique ideas and beliefs, and see things in new ways. We have just scratched the surface in our potential for amazing art, awe-inspiring entertainment, travel through outer space, clean energy, and our health and longevity.

No matter what forces pull us down, internal or genetic, we will succeed, if we follow the truths that lead to our goals.

A plane flies, notwithstanding tons of weight, because its force to uplift is so incredibly strong it overcomes gravity. A plane is made up of thousands of inventions that each may have been "sufficient" for one task (Not associated with the plane), but each one of the thousands is "necessary" to make a plane that flies. Gravity isn't made weaker for the plane to fly; the plane exerted more force and succeeded to fly despite it. The strongest force, or combined forces, win out and determines the direction. With enough understanding, effort and time, anything is possible- regardless of the weight we initially feel or the odds we initially face.

True principles are concepts that can be seen in play in our external world; they explain cause and effect when it comes to the quality of life- for example, honesty. True principles are always in play, just as gravity is always in play, even while a plane flies through the air. Gravity is superseded by a more powerful force, a force sufficient enough to cause it to fly despite its weight. All principles of success, happiness, and the laws of science coexist and are eternal. Despite the gravity of our problems, we can overcome them by the gifts of our humanity and the truths that direct them.

This truism stands immutable, when we live true principles today we can accurately predict clement lives tomorrow. Because of our agency, and our ability to learn and live concepts, we succeed regardless of the rest of our genetics.

<u>Reality- truth- knowledge defined</u>

Reality is things as they are, were, and will be; and truth is an accurate description of anything as it was, is, or can be.

Knowledge is to witness through our senses the reality, and the value of truth. Truth is seen in the details of history, the weather today, or an accurate scientific assessment of what it will be tomorrow.

When we accurately define our words we will see more clearly the relevance of our choices and their effects in our world.

The truth of what will be

For example, where and when will a hurricane develop? If all the science of weather was acquired, and our instruments were precise, then we would not have predictions of the weather tomorrow. Instead of predictions, we would have an understanding of what it will be. The truth of what will bring success in our relationships, our sanity, and our sense of satisfaction in life- reflect true principles, for which we have come to know of their true definitions, and have come to live them.

Whether we make choices violating principles of truth in ignorance, or knowingly, we reap the rewards of violating truth. You may fail to stop at the traffic light but the consequences of that choice do not follow our intent, whether we get a ticket or an accident.

Principles relevant to approximating our potential will affect our lives, whether we have grasped them or not. Any true principle is something that can be examined by our minds because they are seen in play in our physical world. For example, if we are kind to each other and are caring friends to each other, then we will have happy relationships. If we are ignorant of the true need for kindness in our lives, we will suffer the consequences of its lack. The relevance of truth is in play 24/7.

Section 3
Truth is in the details

Science itself is in the study of reality. It is the study of things as they are. The law of identity, which is the first law of all sciences, is

"A=A, and if A does not equal A, then A does not exist. For example, 6 = 1 + 2 + 3. For something to be proven true, everything thing that adds up to accurately describe the subject must also be equal to it. If it is something that exists, then it is something that can be described. Its description is its definition. For example, "This orange is a fruit of the citrus genus. It has an orange color, lots of vitamin C, is sweet…" We are describing the characteristics that are particular to an orange.

The more details we notice and learn about something the more light we have to see and understand it by.

Inductive reasoning

The first practice of seeing and understanding the true nature of things, including our humanity, is in noting the details of its distinguishing characteristics. It is an effort in making an accurate description or account of all things relevant to its identity. We need to find those things relevant to its influence. It is an effort to get all the pieces of the puzzle before we come to any conclusions. Finding the facts that seem to relate to each other, and then looking for a possible theory or opinion that explain them, is called inductive reasoning.

Inductive reasoning creates theories and definitions, while deductive reasoning is to prove if something fits a theory or definition.

Obstacles to sound reason and learning

Pride, closed-mindedness, prejudice, laziness, and judging are hindrances to learning. For example, when we make a final conclusion or judgment, by believing we already know, then we stop learning. Judgments are tempting to make, and negative judgments of others often serve to close our minds, satisfy our egos, or deflect our own indiscretions. Judgments are easy to come by and hard to change.

If we could withhold judgment, if we could just continually fill our minds with the unfolding story or possible theories, we can get an understanding more accurately reflecting reality. More importantly, our world would be a world free of pride and hypocrisy. How much kinder our world would be if we were more interested in understanding than judging?

As long as we are open to new information as possible truths we will grow in understanding and wisdom.

Remaining open to new information is the answer to our rigid and closed minded thinking

Consider the judgment "Jim is a good father," compared to the narrated story, one ongoing and unfolding with details; "Thank you, Jim, for picking up Tommy from school today and helping him with his homework. Tommy told me last night just how much he appreciated your help." The story with its details "shows" us Jim is a good father and also the reasons why. In this example, we can see the power of description and narration instead of opinion and judgment.

Value judgments, good or bad, do not give much information. They also add very little truth value because by themselves they give no evidence, examples, and shows no relevance that brings understanding. Judgments are inaccurate because they are conclusive and definitive about all the virtues and vices we, hold in shades of gray.

Judgments keep us from learning new details

When someone buys a pair of shoes we might ask, "Why that pair of shoes'?" The answer can be as ambiguous as, "Because they are cool," or as informative as "I got this pair because they have closed toes, are orthotic, comfortable, and the heels are not too high which would make it hard for me to walk on them all day. These shoes are the right color for most of my dresses and they are stylish." The first statement is a more popular reason in today's world where judgment is so important. In today's world, we often judge ourselves simply by esteeming ourselves high or low. We also wonder with some anxiety, "How do others see me?"

When people feel inadequate, judging is very natural for them to do. This is a response creates even more vices and causes even more ignorance, which we will discuss later. Judgment simply doesn't lend to rational thinking. "Because they are cool" gives us no reason to add light to why a pair of shoes is chosen. "Because he is cool" gives us no reasons why a person is esteemed highly except he fits into a crowd.

When we are in the habit of making judgments then we do not need a vocabulary or even critical thinking skills. Being in the habit of describing in detail, why things are worthwhile, continually sharpens our minds to the relevant and honest art of persuasion.

The practice of describing in detail is advantageous to our minds to learn to reason for, good taste, good character, beauty, probability, correlation, and cause and effect. The practice of giving details and being precise helps us develop better language skills and vocabulary. With details, we learn to articulate our opinions and share evidence for them. We can further describe things by giving examples others can relate to. This practice of more thoroughly describing benefits those who share their stories and those who hear them.

Describing the details not only helps us better understand what is but imagining as many details better helps are take charge of what can be. Imagine all I can do in an upcoming discussion, or conversation that will help things to be brought out in a more positive and acceptable light. If there is a problem to resolve then I should imagine as many ways of dealing with the problem as possible and with as much detail as possible.

Section 4
Two subsets of truths

Many believe there are different kinds of truth, but the truth is just an accurate description of something the way it is. Whether an accurate definition of an orange or of honesty. For the purposes of this book, we will separate all truths into two main categories. The first is truths descriptive of our tangible world or the laws of physics governing the physical universe. These are not relevant to our human character. They can also include details in the objective narration of events. The second category of truths is descriptive of the concepts that improve the quality of life, specifically truths pertaining to our humanity.

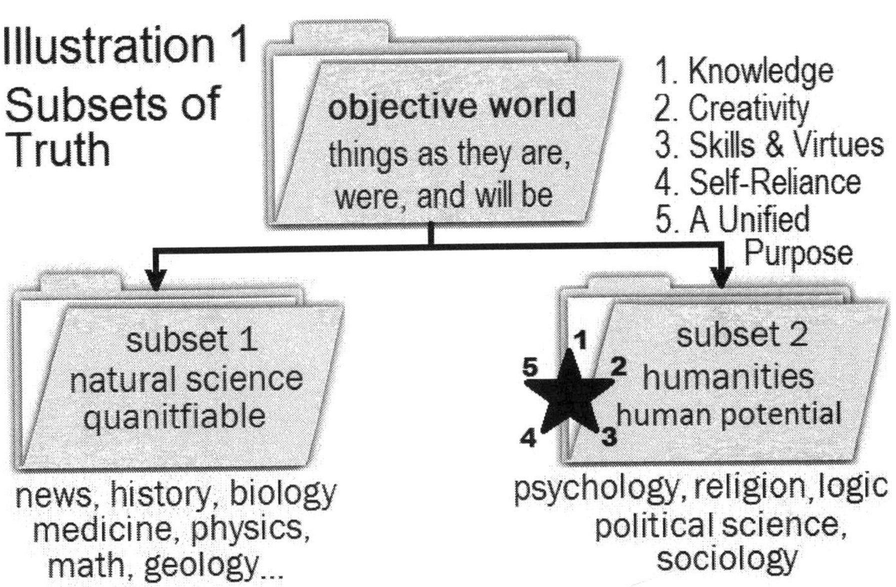

Subset 1) The physical universe

The truths of the physical universe are considered "natural truths." They are the physical properties of the tangible world and the narration of events. We can search for, understand, and then come to accurately describe the characteristics of matter. We can also come to describe or narrate events both present and past as they occurred. Honesty in category one is to accurately describe things as an emotionally unattached observer, with a somewhat inaccurate conceptual tool of representation called language, and with another conceptual tool of quantity and representation called math.

With the natural sciences, if a scientist, news reporter, or a historian stop describing and start embellishing, biasing, or judging-then they stop being objective seekers of truth and they become champions for a particular opinion or agenda.

All truths are inter-operable between all sciences

As each science objectively pursues truth, as each science amasses truth they are ever more inter-operable and synergistic. The sciences will be used together to answer our greatest ambitions. Truths pertaining to the physical world are sought by natural science and earth science. These sciences work with measurable phenomena and laws that depend on accurate quantitative expressions, for example, physics, chemistry, and biology.

Subset 2) All things pertaining to our humanity

We consider these conceptual truths. They are an accurate description of all effectual concepts relevant to both defining and developing human virtue, skill, talent, goals, and happiness. They are the truths relating to the quality of our character and the depths of our happiness.

The humanities department in our schools is concerned with conceptual truth such as psychology, language, and critical thinking. Political science studies how we unite in a common cause to form a nation. The humanities cover the 5 criteria in our North Star, pg. 30. All the concepts of any study of our humanity are susceptible to the laws of logic. Each true concept can be defined and observed in action, they have cause and effect in our objective world.

Fundamental conceptual truths, germane to the gifts of our humanity, direct both categories of truths. They direct our humanity, and our admirable goals for the benefit of our homes, our needs, and happiness.

The description of things intangible

Conceptual truths are discovered by our human ability to think rationally. Without both categories, we could not come to any conclusion Jim is a good father. Conceptual truths are just as reflective of reality as the physical universe and narrative truth. For example, when we saw someone telling the event as it really happened, the name we gave this kind of behavior was honesty. We have learned honesty has favorable cause and effect in our lives. We further observe it is needed to reach our worthy goals and brings us more satisfaction. Because principles are of a moral nature they are easily distorted by our bias, especially by those in which a nebulous morality suits their irrational choices better. If we tell lies a lot, we may prefer a lot of exceptions to our definition of honesty.

Section 5
Logic and the criteria for conceptual truth

Logic is the science to discover the truth through sound reason. The software that allows computers to work properly consist of logic, just like the hardware we call our souls needs logic to live peaceful, loving and happy lives.

A synopsis of the four fundamental laws of logic

1) The law of identity is anything that is must exist in the objective (observable) world. It has an It has an identity which can be observed and defined.
2) The law of the excluded middle is something exist or does not exist. It is either true or it is false. There is nothing in between.
3) The law of causality is everything that exists has an explanation for its existence. Something caused it to be what it is.
4) The law of contradiction is something cannot have two different identities or definitions at any given time.

Faith in truth is not superstition

Any concept proposed as spiritual enlightenment but does not enlighten our minds to understand cause and effect (3rd law of logic) toward reaching our goals, confuses us regarding the efforts which should be made. Faith is not superstition. It requires something makes sense to us before we put the concept to the test-like trying a diet that seems reasonable. Filling our minds with accurate definitions of concepts as they relate to our humanity, holding to the laws of logic, gives a better understanding and a clearer vision of the why's, the how's, and of the reality of what really can be for us.

The criteria for conceptual truth are the gifts of our humanity. For something to be true it must not be antagonistic to these criteria, it must be respectful to our humanity. At the same time, it must be helpful to at least one of them, it is a precept of love. We use the figure the North Star throughout this book to represent our gifts of humanity, our rights, truth, love, respect, and even the guide for a healthy imagination.

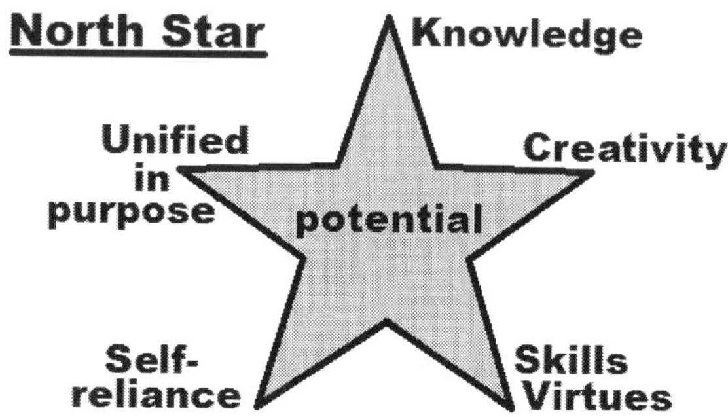

Criteria for truth and love

1) Gaining knowledge: We each have the right to amass and have equal access to information relevant to our lives, to research and come to a greater personal "knowledge" of what indeed is true and what indeed will benefit the path of our personal lives. We have a right to know the truth and to make our own decisions based on what we have experienced and believe, as long as they do not disrespect others boundaries. We have the right not to be deceived. We have the right to be apprised of those choices that anyone makes, that affect the story of our personal lives.

2) Gaining creativity: We have the right to our individuality and self-expression. We have the right to express ourselves in action, dress, and mannerisms as we see fit... again, as long as it is not disrespectful of others. We have the right to build and express this

creative power through talents, craftsmanship, hobbies, relationships, solving problems, getting through trials…etc.

3) Gaining character and admirable skills: We have the right to improve our humanity. Respect allows the equal opportunity for self-improvement, education, and upward mobility within our relationships and society.

4) Becoming self-reliance and remaining free: We have the right to be autonomous, prosperous and to achieve personal independence. We have the right to live where we choose and we have the right not to rely on anyone, or any enterprise, or governing power. We have the right to be free which includes taking personal responsibility and accountability for our needs and the consequences of our choices. We have the right to enjoy the creation of our labors or the earnings of our wages. We have personal ownership of our bodies, our life, and our life's story.

5) Gaining unity and worthy purpose with others: We have the right to associate with others of our choice and to hold a collective purpose. We have the right to live with others of our choice, to develop healthy relationships of reciprocal maturity and autonomy. We have the right to assemble and be unified in a cause, as long as our assembly does not disrespect others rights. This means we do not have the right to block traffic, smear the character of those we disagree with, brake department store windows, and burn flags or burn anything else where pedestrians and cars travel.

These five are the boundaries of our humanity for which we live to have respect and authentic love for each other. These are the truths that guide our lives. These are the "psychological" needs of my well-being and happiness. They do not include our wants, our physical drives, or our appetites. When our freedoms are threatened, whether by lies, manipulations, tyranny…etc., we must choose to protect our possibilities in life or we consign ourselves to a less fulfilling life as well as every generation after us.

Getting to the truth in a world of misinformation can be difficult, but take hope. Most of the claims made against our common humanity, and the potential of the common person, do not even pass simple logic. Everything that is has a cause for its being, and every claim of human concern is relevant to the gifts of our humanity.

Section 6
Critical thinking

Determining the truth of a claim, self-evident truths of our humanity are always relevant

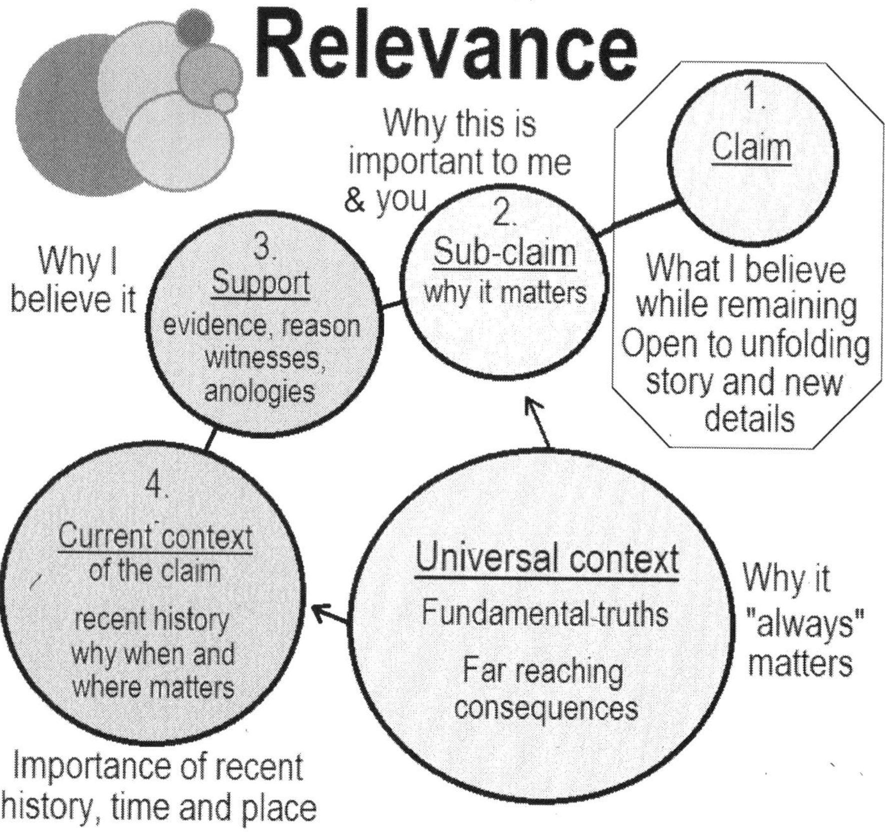

When writing a talk or having a serious discussion this is a good format to follow.

When listening to a claim we should ask questions like these- "Is this relevant to our freedom, our right to think and act for ourselves?" "Is it conducive to our potential by allowing each to take responsibility for one's own gifts?" "Does it allow each to grow by providing for each one's own needs?" "Does it allow us to assemble and unify for the causes or for the beliefs that we have?" "Does it protect the property that our gifts have provided for us?"

Probability is simply the likeliness something is true. Thinking in terms of probability keeps our minds open to new information. Determining probability is easier than coming to a final conclusion. If we have good evidence to believe something is the case, then it is best to express this as probably true instead of making accusations.

Think of something really important that must be discussed in your community, family, or with your neighbor- whether it is politics or religion. This is a good model on the next page to follow. Fill in each step with your story.

Keeping in mind scope, probability, relevancy, opinions, and judgments

In sharing our beliefs, the words we choose can make the difference from being honest and clear, to being senseless. Keeping from exaggerations, which are extreme in scope, is one way to keep the conversation sensible. Words representing scope are: all, every, some, most, seldom, never, any...etc. Superlatives like all, every, none, and never- often make our claims false and tend to show bias, closed minds, prejudice, sexism, manipulations, selfishness, and ignorance.

Section 7
The definition of words

If we are having a difficult time of understanding each other, it is because we are speaking a different language. It may even be that we are speaking both in English and we have different definitions of the words we are using, such as our own separate beliefs of love. And though we all want the same things, such as to belong, be happy, and attain personal success- we believe in different pathways to achieve our goals.

"If you wish to converse with me, define your terms" -Voltaire

Imprecise language: a stumbling block to irrational thinking

The definitions in the dictionary are each word's many contemporary meanings in society. Many keywords of great importance have contradictory meanings. For the purpose of understanding, keywords will be given one definition, in keeping with the fourth law of logic.

We will include all the necessary characteristics of each principle. These definitions are useful to learn and to use in everyday language. They are a way of making our boundaries clear.

Without clearly defined words- law could not be practiced, relationships would not grow, people couldn't unite under a cause, and science would not progress. The more accurate our definitions are, the happier we will be, and the more we will live in harmony. If we define love inaccurately, even when ours and others choices fit our definitions, we will still feel unloved.

Our likelihood of imagining unhealthy or disrespectful ways to get what we desire, increases as our beliefs remain incongruent with each other and incongruent with things as they really are and can be. Some of the words we all hold such different definitions of are: love, objectivity, humility, sympathy, and empathy.

Words, germane to the main ideas of this book, are not defined according to common usage. The definitions of words change with public sentiment and political posturing. We will present definitions that represent human qualities and our objective world. These words will not reflect dictionary definitions. Hopefully, we can infuse into a society an accurate understanding of fundamental human virtues, like yeast that slowly rises the loaf of bread. We need accurate unchanging definitions of virtues. For, human virtues are timeless and unchanging, just as our human potential does not change.

We have perfect vision when we see through glasses of well-defined truths. A discussion of truth is the breaking down of things, as they are, in their true definitions. Love is... democracy is... and then explaining why these characteristics bring us to our potential and happiness.

The meaning of words is so powerful that those who would try to rule the world, have first worked to engineer new words or redefine words. By controlling the media, and public education with well-crafted words they inculcate their political bias into society. These definitions and new words favored their party's designs. It is easy to call the other party racist if we give racism a nebulous and superficial definition.

It is true that there is no language perfectly conducive to rational thinking, making it easier for those who want to manipulate, deceive, and coerce. All the more reason to proactively and objectively define words to hold fidelity to who we are. We need to be proactive a building a free and peaceful world for future generations. Being "Proactive" is to be anxiously engaged in a process of thinking through, and bringing to pass, an admirable end.

Understanding set and subset definitions

The definitions in the dictionary are each word's many contemporary meanings in society. Many keywords of great importance have contradictory meanings. For the purpose of understanding, keywords will be given one definition, in keeping with the fourth law of logic.

We will include all the necessary characteristics of each principle. These definitions are useful to learn and to use in everyday language. They are a way of making our boundaries clear.

Without clearly defined words- law could not be practiced, relationships would not grow, people couldn't unite under a cause, and science would not progress. The more accurate our definitions are, the happier we will be, and the more we will live in harmony. If we define love inaccurately, even when ours and other's choices fit our definitions, we will still feel unloved.

Our likelihood of imagining unhealthy or disrespectful ways to get what we desire, increases as our beliefs remain incongruent with each other and incongruent with things as they really are and can be. Some of the words we all hold such different definitions of are: love, objectivity, humility, sympathy, and empathy.

Words, germane to the main ideas of this book, are not defined according to common usage. The definitions of words change with public sentiment and political posturing. We will present definitions that represent human qualities and our objective world. These words will not reflect dictionary definitions. Hopefully, we can infuse into a society an accurate understanding of fundamental human virtues, like yeast that slowly rises the loaf of bread. We need accurate unchanging definitions of virtues. For, human virtues are timeless and unchanging, just as our human potential does not change.

We have perfect vision when we see through glasses of well-defined truths. A discussion of truth is the breaking down of things, as they are, in their true definitions. Love is... democracy is… and then explaining why these characteristics bring us to our potential and happiness.

The meaning of words is so powerful that those who would try to rule the world, have first worked to engineer new words or redefine words. By controlling the media, and public education with well-crafted words they inculcate their political bias into society. These definitions and new words favored their party's designs. It is easy to call the other party racist if we give racism a nebulous and superficial definition.

It is true that there is no language perfectly conducive to rational thinking, making it easier for those who want to manipulate, deceive, and coerce. All the more reason to proactively and objectively define words to hold fidelity to who we are. We need to be proactive a building a free and peaceful world for future generations. Being "Proactive" is to be anxiously engaged in a process of thinking through, and bringing to pass, an admirable end.

Understanding set and subset definitions

Our beliefs are like a pair of glasses through which we see our world. We naturally see the world through the way we have defined major concepts and virtues, and then categorize things in our minds based on those definitions. Putting things into sets is how we reason. For example, we define what honesty is and then judge people or choices, to be honest, or dishonest, in other words, we put them into sets of honest and dishonest. The problem is, few actually look at how they have defined concepts, and when they do, they do so loosely and with little thought. Whether written down, rational or irrational, aware or unaware- we all make our definitions of concepts and virtues.

In set definitions, the main set is all characteristics that the set members have in common. The set members are subsets. For, each member also has some characteristics that the other members do not have. All things are a part of something else, and all things are unique. Dogs are unique in the animal kingdom, and poodles are a unique kind of dog. Poodles could be our focus, the new main set; toy poodles would be a unique kind of poodle, a subset. No two things are exactly the same.

Understanding set definitions help us to reason. For instance, all dogs are not German shepherds, but all German shepherds are dogs. All things are necessary in some cases (everything in a set may be needed to prove something is the case), and sufficient in others (just one fact can be enough proof).

In the set of virtues belonging to hope we have faith, patience, kindness, and love. Hope is the fundamental definition, and faith, love, Kindness, and patience add more to the definition of hope to define the kind of hope they are. Take away our hope, and then we cannot have faith, love, or patience. Faith is to hope for something to be a true principle, that when acted upon, brings success, well-being, potential, and happiness. Love's first concern is to hope our choices will bring happiness to others because we care about them. Patience is to hope and work until we succeed. Kindness is to act in a friendly, generous, or considerate manner- in hopes of showing care and value of others, and in hopes of keeping peace and unity between individuals.

In the virtues of hope, we are motivated to do worthy things. They are proactive virtues. As in the example of the ship, our agency is the captain, and the crew members are the virtues of hope. Hope is tying down the lines. It is redirecting the sails and throwing out the nets. Hope is looking forward to the day that it drops anchor in safe harbors. The virtues of respect or entrust are the way the captain holds and protect the guests and cargo of the ship. It does so because of their incredible value. This sacred entrustment of the captain envelops the entire world, instilling in the captain joy in the smell of the ocean, the sound of the gulls, beautiful coastlines and the starry nights.

All concepts hold one definition. It makes no difference of whether they used as nouns, adjectives, or verbs, they mean the same thing. If I use respect as a noun and I say that "respect" is of greater worth than admiration, then I am saying that "not crossing boundaries" is of greater worth than having admiration. We can swap the word with its definition. If I use respect as a verb and I say that you should "respect" me, then I am saying that you should "not cross my boundaries."

When we have a false definition of respect mixed in with other definitions, how do we live the true definition? For example, If I believe they have to earn my respect then can I steal from them until I do? How do we treat others differently because people have to earn our respect? If we mean I have high regard for you or a high admiration, then use them. We need a word that means "Do not cross my boundaries". We propose that word should be respected and it should be its only purpose.

The definition of respect around the clear boundaries of human potential will bring more rational thinking than any book on logic or critical thinking could. Respect has the most utility in our lives, for our rational thinking, and for our choices.

Chapter 3: Respect
Building a Place for Love to Dwell

They say the way a relationship begins
Is the way that it will be.
So I begin this journey with eyes wide open
For the ends to see.
Will there be mostly turbulent waters
Or mostly peaceful seas?

Section 1
Respect the highest priority of our humanity

Each of us writes his or her own story, and though each one's story is different, we all hope for love and peace. Deep inside we all want to be great individuals. We all feel the pain of rejection and we all feel a little lost at times. Respect is born by our recognition that we have our humanity in common, and this instilling of respect expands as we treat others with this in mind. Although our stories rarely end as we expected, building our dreams on a foundation of respect is our best chance of making these hopes a reality.

Because we rarely get a glimpse of all we can be, we have not done a great jobs of valuing and protecting each other's worth. We need a greater vision of the potential of every individual.

Each of us is like a note in a song, every note is needed, and every note is of equal value. The generation that can write the symphony of resounding respect permeating its society, will change the course of humanity. The greatest symphony will happen when the true paradigm of respect is thoroughly imbued throughout our world.

Why respect is the foundation of our relationships

We enter our new relationships with bright hope for the future. Even with our best efforts to love and care for each other- most relationships fail, hopes are shattered, and hearts get broken. Why do our stories end up with so many heartbreaks and catastrophes? It is not for lack of hope or the intentions to love. If the same effort had been put in respect for each other, as much as we tried to love each other, our relationships would not only have survived they would have been relationships to be envied.

We really can't discuss the true nature of love unless we first discuss respect. Trying to have a great love, without respect, is like trying to drink from a cup with a large hole at the bottom. Without respect, not even an infatuation would last. We will not feel loved, of worth, or appreciated when we are disrespected. We must, in all our imaginings of what loving relationships will look like, imagine great respect and imagine holding in our hearts a great worth for our partner, so much high regard for each other that love will last a lifetime.

This deep respect becomes more probable when we start and build upon respect, a solid foundation on which we tell ourselves affirmations that build respect and inestimable worth for others. This foundation will hold steady the course of our life's odyssey.

As of present, our divorce rates, just about anywhere in the world, are rising. As I speak with centennials I find the most probable reason is that when they grew up respect for others was more the social norm. See: Respect at school declines, as survey says Greg Toppo, USA TODAY Published 12:01 a.m. ET Jan. 23, 2014 | Updated 10:02 a.m. ET Jan. 23, 2014 https://www.usatoday.com/story/news/nation/2014/01/23/respect-schools-teachers-parents-students/4789283/

It is no wonder why respect is declining in our nation. T.V. sitcoms pushed the laugh button during disrespectful scenes. Rioters are now a paid commodity and are expected to break display windows and loot stores. Movies that appeal to the narcissist, the vengeful, the emotionally inept, those full of profanity and violence, top the charts. Appealing to our worst human appetites is easy to profit for the movie industry. As disrespect rose so did the divorce rate. As art appealed to the worst parts of us we fed the beast. We did not remember who we are. We call this kind of entertainment anti-art, for instead of inspiring us it degrades us.

If one thing in this book were to spread through society and change our world in tremendous and unbelievable ways it would be this definition of respect. Crime would fall to incredibly low rates and happiness would be the new normal.

Respect and its motives are:

A) To choose to think of, regard, speak to, listen to, and treat each person of equal importance to each other and to myself.

B) To choose to not cross the boundaries of someone's: rights, potential, choices, body, or belongings.
C) To choose to not abrasively, deceitfully, or forcefully interfere with anyone's personal unfolding life's story. Respect is not to purposely disturb their peace of mind or slander one's character.
D) To be trustworthy of those worthy promises we have made. (Like wedding vows, or an allegiance to our freedom).

Nothing has brought humanity more misery
Than our treating each other with unequal worth.

Figure 2

Fiats of Respect

Because we hold others' of great worth

1. Be polite and kind.
2. Respect others' bodies and things
3. Don't lie or falsely accuse
4. Do not steal
5. Keep my promises
6. Do not envy
7. Do not hold grudges
8. Listen well to others' stories and viewpoints
9. Do not spread the stories of others' lives
10. Respect others' time, beliefs, and choices

With these ten points of respect, ponder them. What affirmations could I tell myself to better Iremember them and live them? For example, in number 6 I could say, "I will tell myself how happy I am that they have these things." Have a family night where the whole family comes together once a week. This is a time where precepts are taught in the home and then have a fun activity, or a delectable desert served, to make it a night the children look forward to. Each week cover a coule of these ten fiats of respect. Build within them the foundation of successful relationships. Teaching them to never bully others or hurt their reputations, relacing the irreverence for others with a deep regard for the feeling of others.

Building Boundaries

A sense of entrustment is to feel the worth of invaluable things put into our care. This sense of the sacredness or the extreme value for the truth and for others humbles us, builds strong boundaries, and consideration for each other. The depth we can feel for things of extreme worth, even in our imperfect state, determines much of the depth of character we will reach. In all our virtues or vices, we will include the thoughts of such as if they were choices to do the same. To think about stealing from someone is disrespectful. If it is a virtue of entrustment then that sense of sacredness includes our thoughts.

It is humble enough to know
We all have our weakness.
There is no shame in this.
It is respectful enough to know
We are all worthy of high regard.
There is no arrogance in this.

Section 2
The nature of respect

This book puts forward that there are only two virtues, that when defined accurately will cover the gamut of choices in all stages of our lives, which fully prosper and bring genuine happiness to our humanity. These are respect and love. They are always expedient. No matter what other goals or desires tug at our choices if they are not also respectful of others they will be deleterious to our relationships, our happiness, and overall contentment with life. The criteria of respect and love are the wisdom that all things should be done with and they are the spirit of the law. For example, if being honest conflicts with respect or love we choose to love. Like the young child who tells people, they are fat. They don't need to hear it from us.

I have defined love as a choice that prospers our humanity particularly in these five things: individual freedom, happiness, success in worthy pursuits, well-being, and our potential (Gifts, skills, virtue, knowledge). It has to do so without being antagonistic (disrespectful) to any one of them. Love and respect will never conflict with each other for the definition of love includes respect. So, when I mention love it will include respect for those things; but when I mention respect it will not include love. Respect is not the efforts to help in any human pursuit. It is just not getting in the way of our human needs and happiness. Just as all shepherds are dogs, but not all dogs are shepherds. We cannot love and be disrespectful, but we can respect others we even when we do not make extra efforts to love them.

<u>Pairing respect to the essential nature to love</u>

Pairing, for the paradigm of the Gifts of Humanity, is when two virtues or skills "synergize" each other. "The two together are more effectual than the sum of the two separately."

Motives are fundamental beliefs for which drive our choices. A motive to love is the definition we hold of it. If our definition is correct, eventually if we act in congruence to that definition, then we will have the character to love as well. By 14 they should learn respects full definition, feel the weight of its importance, and then begin their new paradigm of love and respect. The motive to love begins here, the capability to love in a perfect world should be well on the way by 16 with a strong work ethic. They should definitely be well on the way to having the character to love by 18-19. This should be our goal.

The set of all the beliefs we have is called a "paradigm." These are the spectacles for which we view the world. Through a paradigm of seeing things we imagine, hope, and choose. Our paradigm can change with the birth of our first child, where, from now on, our priorities change. Big changes like this we call a "paradigm shift." Usually, our change happens very slowly, that is we "assimilate" or adopt a belief that is just a little different than the one we have now. Nearly all of us alter our vision little by little.

Never judge yourself to others or to your past
Never look back for your worth or to the side
Look up! - Look to your potential

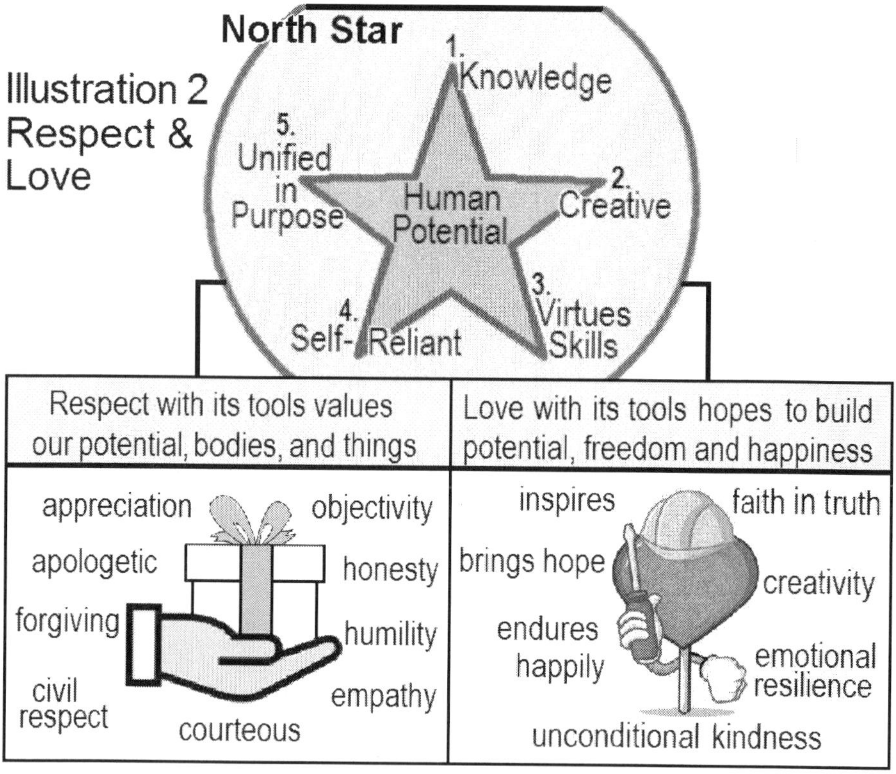

North Star

Illustration 2
Respect & Love

1. Knowledge
2. Creative
3. Virtues Skills
4. Self-Reliant
5. Unified in Purpose

Human Potential

Respect with its tools values our potential, bodies, and things	Love with its tools hopes to build potential, freedom and happiness
appreciation, objectivity, apologetic, honesty, forgiving, humility, civil respect, empathy, courteous	inspires, faith in truth, brings hope, creativity, endures happily, emotional resilience, unconditional kindness

When it comes to their behavior, children should be taught mostly respect. Respect should be their paradigm. They should know that respect is how we regard and treat ourselves and others. For each of the fiats of respect, we can say, "How would you feel if this happened to you?" "Isn't he or she as important as you are?" Much of what you keep reminding them will become their own affirmations.

If our children mature as they should, by mid-teens their paradigm should start including love. They should have a greater focus on making a difference in life. They can be mature enough to understand the definitions of respect and love- as well as the wisdom behind them. In a more spiritually (driven by purer motives) minded world, this would be about 14 years of age. By 16 years of age, they should be ready to handle many adult problems. If we teach them early enough and well enough, even in our modern world, they should be ready to leave home by 17-18 years old. Their vision of life and what life expects from them should be in high fidelity.

The young adult paradigm.

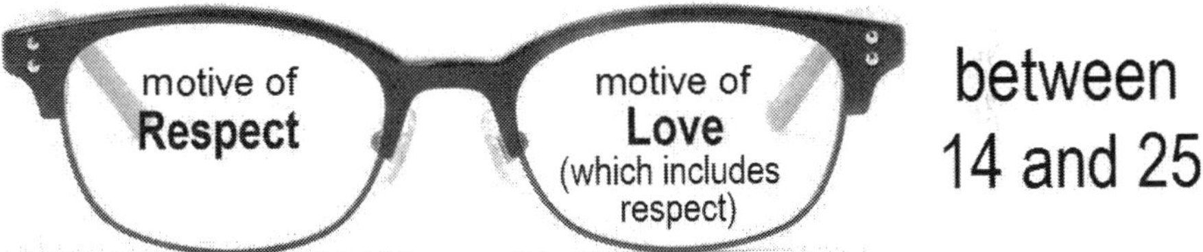

If they remain humble and have good listening skills, somewhere in their mid to late twenties, they will be motivated by empathy as much as they are by love. For the final paradigm, 25 years of age and up, see chapter 4 section 7. The final paradigm includes empathy.

And though youth can care about the pains of others (love) they still have a long way to go before they really can closely approximate and feel the pains of others (empathy). The complete set of boundaries that separate you and I take time and maturity to develop.

Love and respect are a paired duo, like goals that have the near same interest, they uphold and strengthen each other. Like the goal to lose weight, the goal to exercise, and the goal to count calories. Love and respect should be their paradigm by the time they leave home. Even the careers they are seeking should be sought to be a service to humanity.

<u>A subjective world congruous with "who we are"</u>

In regard to a healthy and effectual internal world, we will coin a term and call it "intra-congruous." The word congruous will always have the added implication of being true to "Who we are." Its congruous efforts will be reflective of deep respect and genuine love. Intra will always refer to within the mind. We must remember we answer our needs and fulfill our lives by the gifts of our humanity. The continuous efforts, for intra-congruous harmony with "who we are," is the refining fire that all we must go through to having a loving and respectful character.

The term intra-congruous will be defined as:
A) All subjective faculties: desires, moods, emotions, imagination, creativity, and thinking are compared to our potential in efforts to plot a course to further approximate that potential.
This self-honesty leads to a humbling of the self.
B) Its motive is cognition aimed at creating clean and directed thought, choice, goals, harmony with others, and building happier lives.

Section 3
The teaching and modeling of respect

Relationships pose a challenge for us to rise to and are beyond the ken of young children, whereas respect can be taught at a younger age to prepare them. The blueprints of respect are easy to understand. They should simply be taught to "not" interfere with others' things, their bodies, or say mean things about them. They should be taught good manners and being kind by parents and elementary school teachers. They should learn this by the age of eight.

By the age of 12, "We" and "Us" should be said as often as "I" and "Me". The words, "I want" and "It isn't fair" should put up red flags in their minds. They need to know they are not the center of the universe. They should also know that they shouldn't worry about what everyone else thinks about them. They need to know, though they may feel unprepared for life, this is normal. They should have learned some patience with themselves. They can start taking more satisfaction in hard work and in a job well done.

Also by the time they are twelve, they should be mature enough to let go of friends that are not learning to respect and choose friends who are. They are not naïve children anymore; can they let go of their childhood friends that are becoming bullies and are headed for future incarceration. Letting go of some friends and finding new ones is a difficult thing to do, but they should be taught that making hard choices is what it means to become an adult. Though no mountains are climbed, in the path motivated by self-respect, it takes a brave soul to change friends. Let them know how proud you are of them.

They should be taught that our nation's laws are about respect; for example, not stealing, vandalizing, and that by obeying the traffic laws we all get to work and school safely.

Before they start dating by sixteen they should know, “Before I give what is most sacred, my life’s story and my body', each must show me that he or she is trustworthy and can give me unconditional respect." Sacred, defined for purposes of being true to “who we are,” would be anything of inestimable worth. The ramifications of dating are so personally impacting as to require that each party holds a deep respect for each other.

If they will not be wise about their friends at 12 they won’t be wise about who they choose to date. Not even by sixteen are juveniles ready to try to fix the lives of others. It will be much harder to inspire them at sixteen, to make the right choices, than at twelve. Hopefully, they will learn to stand in respectful places, because of the healthy activities there and the high-regard each has for others attending.

Join the few on the path true to "who we are"
And invite everyone else to come along

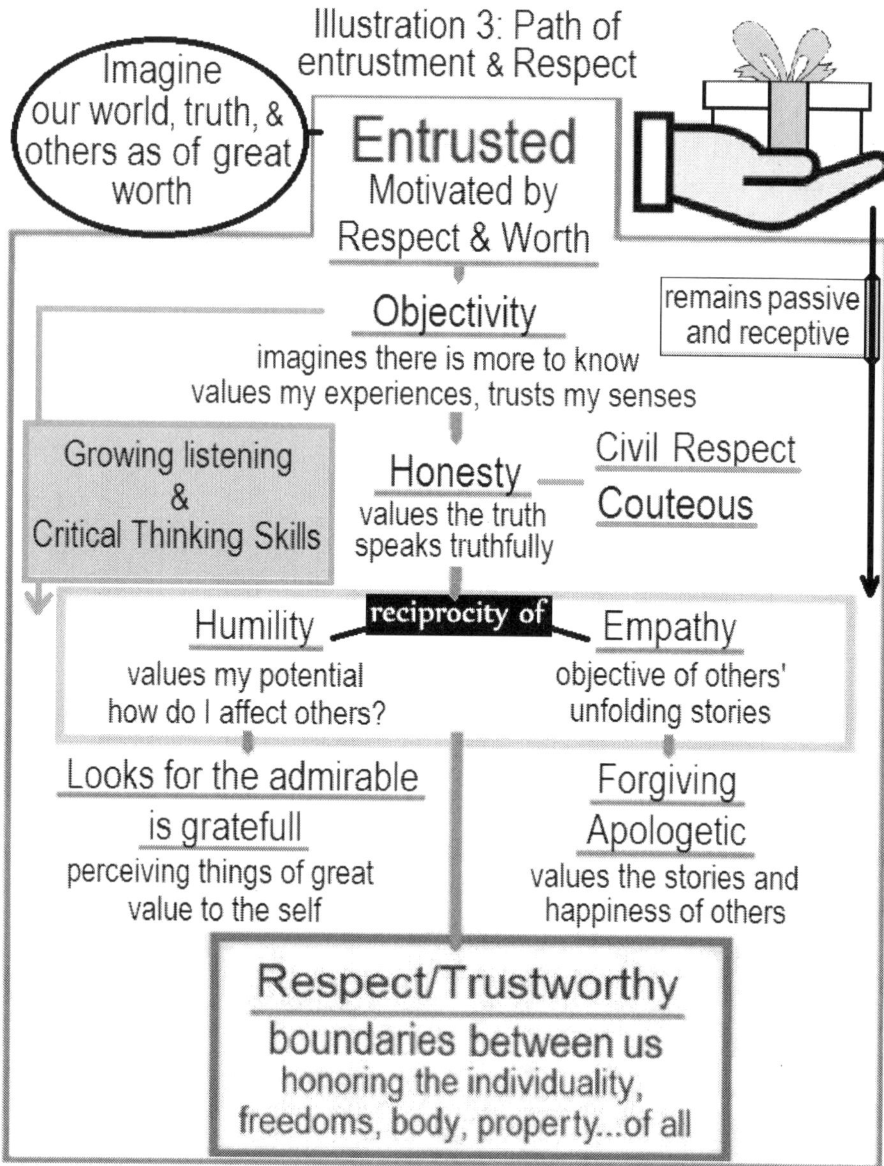

Model respect

The best way we can teach a child to respect others is to show respect for them, especially when, we discipline them. We don't scream, demean, or purposely disturb their peace of mind. We don't use violence and disrespect their bodies. We withhold privileges, place in the corner, and we give long quiet sermons. I promise they will hate the sermons and they will learn true principles. We are not "asking" our children to behave, we are informing them that we will not tolerate disrespect. And as we show them respect, through the course of our lives, we are teaching them and influencing them beyond the influence of words alone.

Just like appreciation can run deep, the sense of holding something as sacred in our hearts also can be deep and intense. This idea is quite alien in our so-called world of sophistication and science. But this holding each other deeply with great worth is needed for our happiness. Just how skilled can someone be in a sport or playing an instrument? Even of greater importance, just how much can we hold one another with great worth?

Section 4
The grass is greener

These next 15 possibilities are ways we disrespect each other and are listed as variations to the tale of the green grass. These are just some notable examples. There is an indefinite number of ways we could be disrespectful. It is best not to think of these as categories of people but thinking errors we may have developed.

1) Trying to prove who is better or that the other is worse in a relationship (Pride) *At least my grass is greener than yours.*

This is the, "You are not so good yourself game," or the, "At least I am better than you are game." These statements are not quantitative certainties, they are not provable. They truly are born of a discordant imagination. This is true with all of the fallacies we will present using the green grass.

With respect, a relationship should never be a competition between individuals who are fighting for their egos. We are on the same team where each builds the other up.

2) Trying to prove who is more hurt in the relationship (Self-righteous pity) *My being more emotional about my dead grass is my proof that I am the bigger victim.*

In this competition feelings are usually weapons of proof that the other has done wrong, or that the other needs to try harder, or feel sorrier. This is a battle that often runs simultaneously with the, "You are not so good yourself" game. One may heighten their anger, and the other may choose to break down and cry. It is a fight of self-righteousness and self-pity. I can be angrier than you. I can cry louder than you.

3) The grass will be greener when I am in someone else's yard (Ingratitude/envy/lust)

These are those who are not grateful for the blessings that they already have, and they are not working on making their grass greener. They think others just have a better yard to play in. Many, who want out of a relationship, begin building emotional distance by finding fault and giving themselves excuses to be harsh.

4) Not taking responsibility for caustic emotions (Immaturity/poor judgment/lacking skills to answer one's own challenges) *You're the reason the grass isn't green enough.*

The, "I'm blaming you for my boredom, sadness, being disgusted, anger... What are we saying when we are easily bothered or bored with someone? Who is responsible for my emotions, like my anger? Am I so unimaginative and un-creative that I need someone else to entertain me? Or that I need someone to keep me from falling apart, or keep my life bump free?

When I find someone unhappy in a relationship and desires to enter a new one with me, it is probable that I will be unhappy with me as well.

5) A fixation on fairness and equality of things (Fairness, envy or jealousy, leading to force or manipulation) *It isn't fair the grass is greener in your yard.*

I'm going dig up some of the grass from your yard and plant it in mine, or I'm going to kill the grass in your yard so we can be equal.

This person may be motivated by jealousy desire to take away someone else's happiness. Fairness thinking is easily prone to feel self-pity. These are also those that are motivated to make things fair. "I'm going to teach you a lesson."

6) Showing disgusts for simple unintended mistakes or perceived mistakes (Arrogance) *It bothers me your grass isn't green enough.*

These will judge you without thought. They are too arrogant to realize that their grass is not so green. When in relationships, they are annoyed or angry over the smallest winds of discomfort. They are constantly finding or imagining fault over the most trivial of things.

Blaming others for my feelings is the
Most common form of disrespect.

7) Controlling a relationship by demanding personal information from others and not disclosing information about the self (Insecurity/control) *If the other doesn't see my dead lawn, or if I simply deny having a dead lawn, then I can demand that the other's lawn is made greener.*

It is disrespectful to demand personal information from someone. Having all the information may seem like a drug of power to the controlling party, having all the weapons of judgment and hidden indiscretions. But it is a lonely road of unsatisfying relationships and rarely being appreciated.

8) Instead of accepting personal weakness and taking responsibility we find pleasure in the others faults. (Psychotic tendency) *I'm excited about your grass dying because I feel better about myself when I do.*

9) Not giving adequate time before choosing to be more serious in a relationship (Neediness) *I hadn't noticed that my glass lenses are tinted green so when I find out that your grass actually needs the same loving care as everyone else's then I am disappointed.*

These have projected their hopes onto someone and see them through their assumptions but not the real person. These people embellish romantic moments and live in a word of fantasy. Their new flame could be no more than a manikin, would they notice? For a few months all they see is the good in someone, and then for the next few months, all they see is the bad.

10) Unrelated criteria for entering or remaining in a relationship with others (Being superficial/insecure) *What matters most is that everyone else thinks my grass is the greenest, you are with me to help me keep up the illusion.*

When looking for suitable relationships, many will look at what kind of car someone drives. The one they want must be tall, weigh only so much, have this color hair, hold this figure, have this hobby, play an instrument, work in this field, drive this kind of car, eat this kind of food, where this style clothes, etc. Even after meeting a checklist of superior cosmetic wants, the times and fashions will change. The message is you are here to help me keep up with appearances. I never notice this life never brings me any real satisfaction, it's just around the corner.

11) What is in it for me personally? (Selfishness) *Your only function in life is to make my grass greener.*

Self-centered people expect and then demand a lot from others. As a self-centered person, I would expect others to make their choices based on my wants and by the way that I am used to things.

12) The tendency to be a reactionary person instead of being a person of character (the chameleon, lack of character, lack of personal identity) *I would make my grass greener if my surroundings were green already.*

Respect, like love, is a character trait. It is not a response to other's choices, or to life's good fortune. If I cannot be respectful when I am in a bad mood, then I am simply not respectful. If I cannot be respectful when others are not respectful towards me, then I am not respectful. Rather, I am a chameleon whose lack of character takes on the moods, sentiments, or attitudes of those around me.

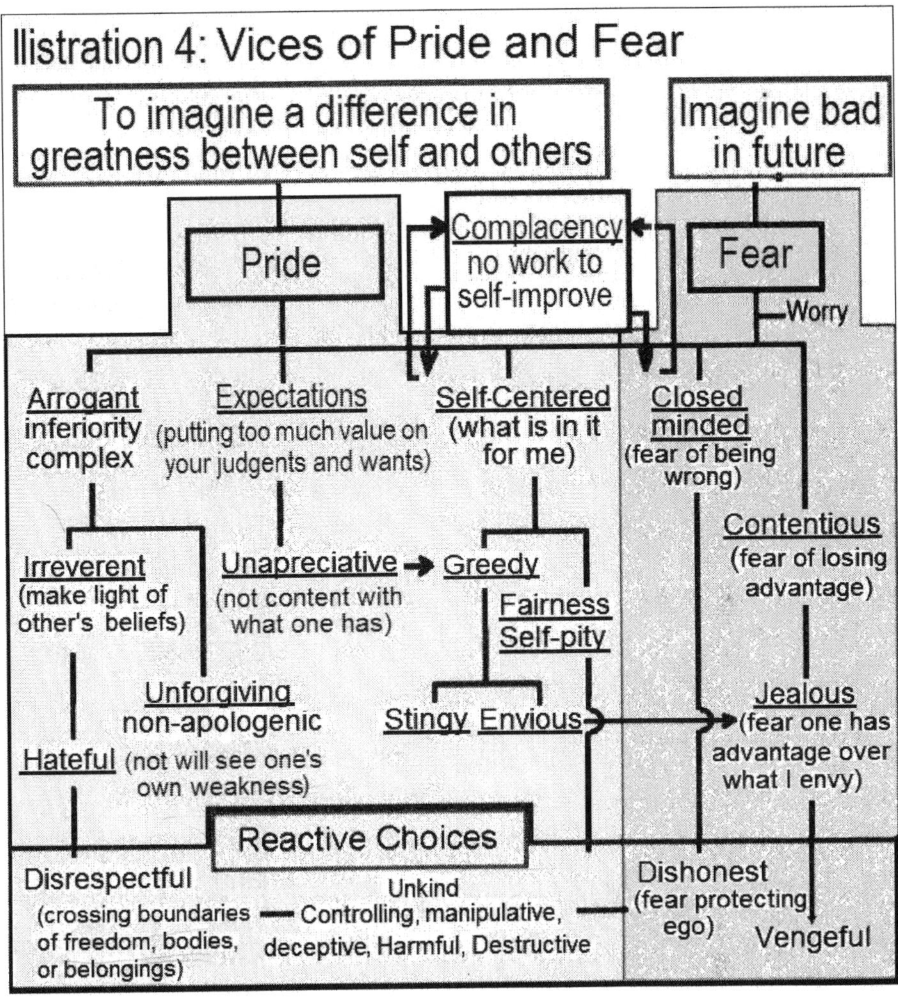

(In illustration 4, arrows pointing to complacency represent being compelled to be humble, like getting caught, and then quickly losing the guilt that once humbled us. Complacency can be analogous to a man who jumped off a ten-story building without a parachute and as he passed the fifth floor he was heard to say, "Everything is alright so far." This illustration focuses on the negative, as these analogies of the green grass do. But it is in the efforts to climb higher we move forward and keep from the ugly consequences of not being true to ourselves. Complacency will end with the same story as apathy does, or pride or selfishness does.)

13) The tendency to find fault, nag, put others down, and feel sorry for ourselves (the miserable nag) *I'm going to punish you with my emotions throw a tantrum, teach you a lesson, remain sad or mad until you make my grass greener.*

Some people are simply negative. Some people use hard to bear emotions to punish or control others. But instead of this being a reactionary trait, as in #11, these are negative near all the time. Finding fault feels good to them. Preaching, nagging, and showing a lack of confidence in others just comes naturally.

14) Getting my identity at the expense of my children's freedoms *My child's green grass is a reflection of how great I am.*

Do we over-identify with our children to build our own ego? Do we allow them to make choices within the abilities of their stage of life? Do we feel like a failure when our children fall short? Are we letting them write their own life's stories? Do we let them take accountability for their choices?

15) The desire to tell the story that belongs to others (pride and gossip) *Did you know the neighbor's grass isn't green?* (Implying and instilling the belief that my grass is greener by the comparison)

Vice and complacency

Our humanities courses and behavioral science courses in our colleges study the reactionary person. Most of us are reactionary, probably as much as 90% of us. Few of us are actively working on our character. Being a balanced and poised person of character is not what our modern society esteems. Using our imagination in hope and in entrustment, are not even considered. This is to some degree, keeping humanity from reaching higher levels of personal and societal possibilities.

The memes that can spread through our societies, making respect about human boundaries and which shows its nature to be unconditional, are the answer.

Chapter 4- Love
The Motive to Make the Difference

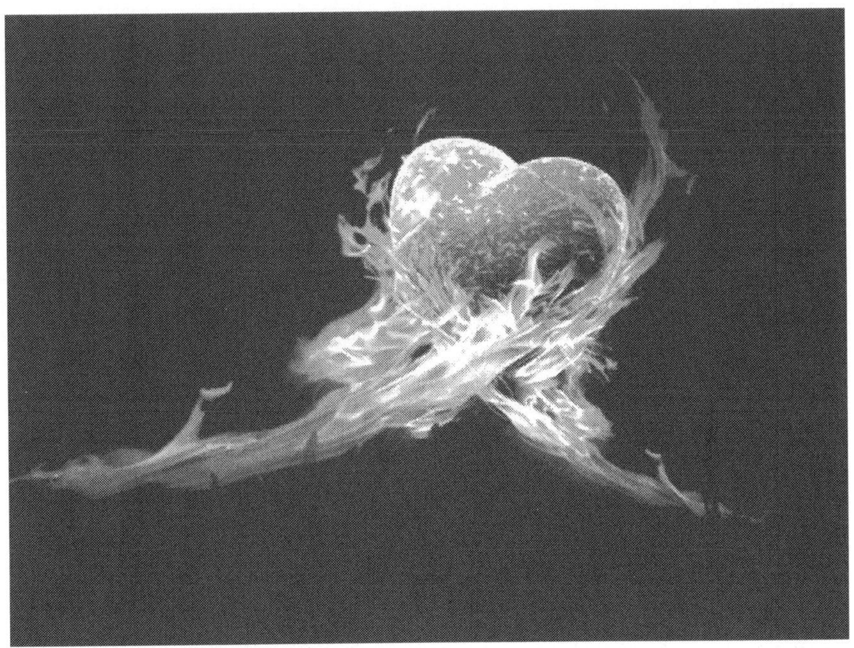

Melted in a furnace, impurities burned
Place in a mold, cooled to form
Super-heated and forged, features cast
Burnished and polished, ready at last.
In the severity of life, love can refine
The character fashioned in its design

Section 1
The nature and utility of love

Love is that virtue and motive that brings to our world those things we have come to believe are most sublime and central to our happiness. And though love can be elusive and mysterious, it's truly something that this world desperately needs more than ever. We need it to be prevalent in our daily lives, guiding our every choice, and motivating us to do great things. Its influence is needed not just for happy relationships, but for peaceful communities and thriving nations.

Its influence includes the feelings that tug on our hearts, such as the excitement we feel with the triumphs of our loved ones, or the panic that grips us when we see them suffering. Love's influence connects us and binds us to each other. We can feel the very strength of these bonds. Like when a father sees his young child scrape a knee and then hears the cry for daddy. Or when the friend, we have learned to admire and endear, whispers in our ear for the first time, "I Love you'.

In a world where love is so misunderstood, where both children and their parents take so long to grow up, we have the dilemma of those who are children "in emotional quotient" raising children. Those who are behind emotionally cross boundaries that weaken the bonds that unite them. The chaotic atmosphere of parents without boundaries prematurely strip the innocence of the children.

A three-year-old may have the desire to drive a car but lacks the ability to do so. The test drive alone would be catastrophic. Many get involved in serious relationships but lack the ability to cope and care for each other. The relationship is catastrophic to each partner. Loving motive and love itself are not the same things, any more than the desire to drive the car is the same thing as driving the car. We have to see our failure, not as failures of love, but as failures from not holding the boundaries of respect and having ambiguous and false definitions of love.

"I am still learning." – Michelangelo

Illustration 5: The path of love- Bulding things of worth

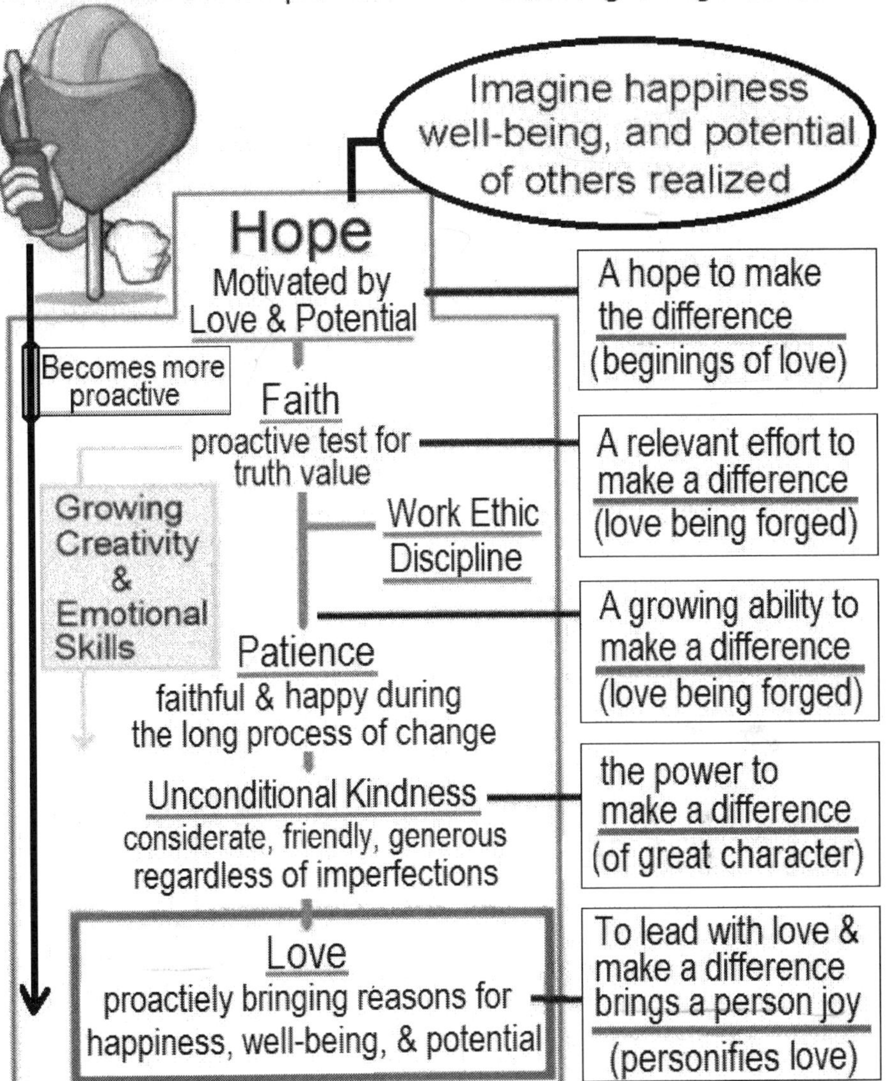

To better see a correlation and progression of proactive virtues a simple definition does wonders.

1) Hope: to anticipate a better future.
2) Faith: test truths that would lead to a better future.
3) Patience: to be happy while we ~~wiath~~ wait for a better future.

4) Unconditional kindness: being friendly and generous, bringing others a better today.
5) Love: efforts to bring more happiness, success, and potential.

Though each one of us is of immeasurable worth, for us to really enjoy our lives these virtues have to blossom if we are going to see our potential blossom. In this life we are not just taking a short test drive in our neighborhood, we want to see the world as it is and really can be. Only love can bring our potential and worth to life that is so latent within us. With love people come together, not to compete and tear each other down, but to synergize each other's efforts. They help build each other's character and celebrate their world together.

In our efforts to build each other and enjoy life are two specific mindsets (motives). Of 1) respect for the wroth of others leading to acceptance and understanding. With the eyes of empathy, we see into the soul of others. We will listen, refrain from bias and remain open to an unfolding story. And with the heart of 2) love, we will hope and care enough to do whatever it takes to bring out the best in others. All choices should be based on a faith in truth and in the wisdom of "who we are."

This duo of holding things admirable to be of worth and the hope to realize that worth, leads away from complacency. No one, who lives a life of caring for the happiness of others, will be complacent in life. Fire is constantly burning within them, driving them to make a difference in life. They are experiencing the compassion of empathy and love and the delight of seeing human achievement and joy. The deep and seemingly unimaginable appreciation for my spouse, cheering with his joys and wiping away his tears of sorrow- this is finding joy in the meaning of my creation.

Regardless of the fact that love will always be an abstraction for the philosophers to debate, we can demystify it. We can, with an ever-improving effort, make love an integral part of our life.

Love and its motives are:
A) Efforts to bring self and others to their potential.
B) Because of our choices brings reasons for happiness, harmony, and unity in our relationships and must be paired with mutual respect.
C) The wisdom and manner by which all concepts, virtues, skills, talents, sciences, cooperative efforts, powers, governments...etc., are deployed for the benefit of our personal character, our relationships, communities, nations, and our humanity. Antonym: Disrespect.

Without exception, the wisest choice is the most loving

Most of what is good in our lives come from our efforts to have faith, patience, and love- The proactive virtues

Good doesn't come to us in our lives because we stopped doing horrific or bad things. It comes because we were true to "who we are." Things of true worth grace our lives by making good choices. Things of worth in relationships comes from generous souls who "want" to go the second mile- those who want to love more. A desire to improve life and relationships. If we can't find deep satisfaction in life, it isn't because we failed to stop hating, it is because we failed to start loving. Love is not just the absence of hate, it is a deep concern for the quality of life and the welfare of others. Love's biggest stumbling block is to become complacent with ourselves.

Complacency is: to lack desire for self-improvement or to lack a desire to finish a job to one's best ability.

(In figure 3 the tools of love are proactive. They build within us as natural consequences to the efforts to live by love's true definition. They are used to accomplish love's designs (definition). We need the right tools to reach our potential or inspire others to their potential. For example, trying to get others to reach their potential without being kind is like doing brain surgery with a hammer.)

Figure 3: Love is proactive–It creates and serves

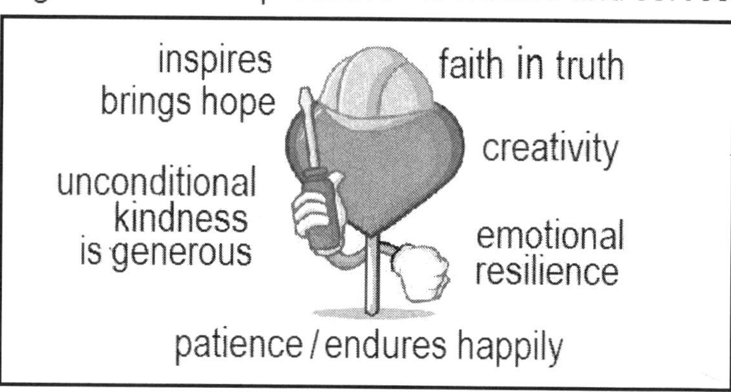

Pairing virtues of hope with those of entrustment

These two mindsets (motive of love and respect) synergize each other, we will call this union, to combine them in purpose, "pairing." Just as caring, about the worth of others, helps us to love them, knowing that others love us allows us to more freely put our care into their hands. "They do not care how much you know until they know how much you care."-Anon. Love, which hopes to make a difference in someone's life story, must be placed with respect- No one wants us prying into their lives, even when we offer to help unless he or she is held important in our eyes. People are more likely to make the effort of painful rehabilitation, and endure the difficult therapy of life, if they feel loved and of worth.

If we cannot love others the way they are,
Love will always be beyond our reach.

The power of love

We tend to measure power by its destructive force in a moment in time. Is that ultimate power a supernova, or a black hole? As powerful as stars and black holes are, they will eventually die. We often vilify humanity for its destructive choices to our planet. But then, mankind alone has the potential to save our planet from natural forces that will eventually destroy it, such as comets, rogue planets, black holes, asteroids, an expanding older sun, or solar flares.

In the past decade, while we are still in the incipient beginnings of technology and science, we have created devices that create the conditions of a star. We have built super-particle colliders to understand particle physics and the origins of the universe. We are moving towards becoming able to travel to distant worlds.

Regardless of the destructive forces that vie to push us off course or destroy us, they are ultimately only a challenge for our humanity. No matter the scope of our problems love can overcome them. Our motivation to love has inspired us to learn and invent and to save us from disease and catastrophic disasters.

If nature has an end, a universe that expands its energy grows cold, then dies- then nature's creation of humanity is its hope for everlasting life. Our human ability to pull together, to answer our challenges, and to care for and love each other has no limits- with enough time, creativity, and continual effort.

-Purpose-
Inspire me to believe and reach.
Hold priceless my soul.
Let nothing hold us back,
In the story that we make together.

Bonds of love and worth- Holding tight to the ones we love

How do we keep those we love in our lives? Obviously, they have their agency but we can do much to entice them to always remain by our side. We can do much to keep our children faithful to those things we taught them and have them keep us close to their hearts. The bonds that keep us together are built from 4 different influences. 1) Being held of worth by keeping good boundaries from the motive of respect. 2) Being understood from listening skills and the power of empathy. 3) Being cared about by the constant effort to love and each other, putting their happiness and well-being in the highest priority. And 4) Being cherished and appreciated by giving and receiving humble gratitude.

Section 2
Losing hope is losing self-love

Love and overcoming weakness (self-love)

If we instill in others the belief that no amount of effort can cause the needed change to overcome their weakness, then we take away their ability to love themselves. When we take away their belief that it is possible we take away hope, and their motivation to change. We must remember that faith, patience, kindness, and love are subsets of hope- they are different kinds of hope. If the main set of dogs became extinct, you would also not have the subset of dogs, like poodles, shepherds, terriers…etc.

Taking away hope, or the sense of something's worth is at the heart of spiritual abuse in these two mindsets. There is no, "You or I can't," in love. There is no "You or I am broken (of less value) in respect. There is just work to do to complete ourselves. There is no "You should be ashamed of yourself," or, "I should be ashamed," in respect. Who among us is sinless enough to cast the first stone of public censure? There is just work to do to make better choices. Love encourages and stokes its fire of hope to burn hot enough for all to enjoy.

Our answer to spiritual abuse is in affirmations like, "There is nothing 'wrong' with me, or you." "I am simply a human becoming." "You and I can do anything with just more time and effort." "And, the greater the bad habits are that must be overcome, the more and the longer it will be that love is needed."

Imagination that builds love and healthy boundaries

Our "agency" is never broken therefore I am never broken. Agency is always in full force, everything subjective (Moods, attractions, desires, emotions, and thoughts) is subservient to it, they are giving us information to use on our behalf. The fear and believe I am broken or can't help myself is, in itself, a very destructive thought to entertain.

If I am attracted to things that can't bring me the joy and happiness that I deserve, then I need to learn to admire those things that do- I need to imagine those things that are of greater worth to me, I need to imagine them in a more favorable light. Everything has its time and place under heaven, even sarcasm (not aimed at people but our own choices). Learn to use the greatest faculty we have, imagination, to aid in changing what we have become to be closer to who we should be.

At the heart of love is the faith to change
A faith that can move mountains

Everyone will make different mistakes, that is not being broken, that is being human

We are not always going to make all the right choice even when we try. As humans, we simply will make mistakes and entertain unhealthy choices. But the tendencies we have are like the wind blowing, the direction we take is a matter of choice and character built through time. The most productive efforts are built around the boundaries we have built through time. The imagination that something is wrong with me is false and leads to even more entrained destructive behavior. We may have things to apologize for but we don't need genetic engineering or drugs because we think we are broken. It is disrespectful to tell others there is something wrong with them. We simply all have different things to learn. This is not a flaw but a challenge we share in humanity.

I find when I am doing a task, for which a good job or a complete job is impossible, I do not put a tremendous amount of energy into it. I may do enough to feel satisfied with my effort but nothing more. When I do a job for which I know can be done 100%, even if it is very difficult over time, then I put everything I got into it until it is accomplished. This is the power that hope brings; this is the power that love has.

Section 3
Expressions of love

Happiness- The more you give it away,
The more it becomes your own.

Love is spoken in many ways to bring cohesion and inspire us

Love motivates and says I love you in many ways. It determines how I treat others, and how I care for them in my heart. After we imagine and affirm how important others are, we are a step closer to holding them as important in our hearts and telling them how important they are.

Love expresses itself in many ways and says that you matter, you mean the world to me- like an embrace that holds tight and waits for the other to let go first and eye contact that holds more steadily and is slow to look away first. I feel genuine loved by the smile that comes to life because someone sees my face, or with the touch on my hand, or when I love you is said sincerely. Love is felt when you show patience after I lost your keys, left my phone behind, or forgot to turn the stove off. Love is the motive behind the patience that says you are worth more than any possession that I could possibly have. Love shows others that their feelings of worth, acceptance, and being loved are worth more than any inconvenience.

Love accents the good in others by appreciation and admiration

Love should be expressed by an appreciation as much as it is in any other way. This is even a more direct expression of valuing someone. For example, "Thank you for listening to me and trying to understand me. Thank you for being such a kind and patient friend especially when I'm so difficult at times. I'm so fortunate that I have such an amazing son that is always doing your homework, cleaning your room, doing your chores, and being a good example to your sister'. These are the generous words that we are blessed to hear when we have others that love us. These bring unifying bonds of love. We can overlook the small petty things we all fall short in and complement the good things we do.

The expressions of love
Are in all the endless kind and little things
That add up.

Kindness is: to act in a friendly, generous, or considerate manner- regardless of the imperfections of others in hopes of showing care and bringing to the other a sense of being valued. Unconditional kindness is that expression that loves people the way they are.

Kindness the greatest tool of love

Before we can love unconditionally we must learn to be unconditionally kind. This doesn't mean we let others disrespect us, it just means that whatever we must do we do so with as much kindness as possible. Unconditional kindness means that even if we are treated unkindly by others we never will lose hope for them, their happiness and potential. Kindness is a generous portion that brings more hope to others, especially to those who need it the most.

We can truthfully affirm, "If I do not treat them kindly, I am not treating them with love." Our lofty goal is to ultimately obtain that virtue which is the apex of who we are…one who personifies love. Kindness is a loving act that can be simple but takes less wisdom then love… an act even young children can understand and always do.

When we are kind we are more concerned about being generous and loving, we are giving someone more than their fair share. Kindness signature characteristic is generosity. We may give more love and forgiveness than what others might consider a proportioned response. Kindnesses generosity reaches out hoping for things of greater value than a proportioned response.

Though we cannot make others happy, love is a promise to bring "reasons" for true happiness, both now and for always. That we are in the habit to think first before I speak. Are these thoughts reflective of our better selves? Do they consider the others worth? When spoken would they give the other even greater hope? Or are they condescending and meant to bring guilt and emotional pain?

What a generous love most looks like

Each time we choose to be believing when things seem hard, each time we choose to have a good attitude - we are expressing love. Bringing hope back into our lives or the lives of others is a work of love. Giving kindness when we are exhausted, overlooking the mistakes of others is an act of love. Finding things to be grateful for when we felt slighted is an expression of love.

The "depths" of our love can't be measured in our clement times. It is best seen and turbulent winds and stormy seas. Its true nature and depths comes to light when it is needed most.

Section 4
Human greatness

Greatness is embodying the gifts humanity intended for us to develop, its primary characteristic is kindness. True love reaches for and embodies those things that are admirable about humanity. Unfortunately, our society has changed what they find to be great in an individual. Where, in the recent past, Helen Keller or Winston Churchill were esteemed as great individuals for their greatness in character. Today a pop star, a movie star, or a talented athlete is held in highest regard. Those we esteem the most are those we try to emulate. Few today have a strong hunger to grow in character. Their desires are about being popular and liked, without facing hard choices. We have various reasons why we might esteem someone to be great, hopefully, those things we value are true to who we are.

When things are hardest to bear, when our patience is tried, when our pride is pricked- this is where the crucible of love is tested and proven- this is when who we are can shine its brightest.

Love, that character trait that brings reasons for happiness, truly is the greatest of character traits that one can possess. To love in ways that make a difference in the lives of those around us takes work and a great deal of time. Here one must be brave even when unpopular. Being able to lift, inspire, and improve no matter the weight of the challenge. The greatest love betters the self, leaving ripples of change through time.

Illustration 6: The Pairing of Entrustment and Hope

To imgine as sacred and of inestimable worth: the truth, our world, and others.
North Star
Knowledge
Unified in Purpose
Human Potential
Creative
Self-Reliant
Virtues Skills
To imagine the potential, well-being, & happines of self & others realized
Remains passive and receptive
Entrusted
Motivated by respect & worth
Hope
Motivated by love & potential
Becomes proactive
Pairing
Objectivity
Imagining there is more to learn valuing my experiences
Faith
Proactive effort in testing for truth value
Growing listening and critical thinking skills
Honesty
values truth speaks truthfully
Civil Respect
Courtesy
Work Ethic
Discipline
Growing creativity & emotional skills
Humility
reciprocity of
Empathy
compares to potential how do I affect others?
Values the unfolding story of others
Patience
fathful & happy during the long process of change
looks for the admirable
is grateful
perceives things of great value to the self
forgiving
apologenic
values others peace of mind and happiness
Unconditional Kindness
considerate, friendly, generous regardless of imperfections
Respect/Trustworthy
having strong boundaries with our things, body & freedom
Love
proactively bringing reasons for happiness, well-being, & potential

We often determine greatness by a singular extraordinary accomplishment, but it is in the abundance of the seemingly common and consistent loving choices that determines greatness.

Examples of the ordinary that add up are the child that honors and respects his or her parents, a student that always does her homework and keeps her GPA up consistently through time. This is true with the young man that keeps away from the gangs and drugs, works his way through trade school, and then chooses a good partner. We admire the man who provides for his family and shows them, love. Great is the husband that respects and treats his wife like a queen, never speaks harshly to her, and continually finds things to praise her for. The wife that sincerely says I love you and it's alright, who is kindly patient when her husband says he is too tired to help out around the house. We are proud of the mother that successfully teaches her children to be polite, honest, hardworking, and kind.

Principles of human greatness are best instilled in the family. It takes a lot of time, just one step at a time, for great things to happen. It takes people who are committed for the long hall, and who are emotionally invested.

Greatness is remembering that one we are angry at, is also the one that needs our understanding. Often it is the one we promised to honor and cherish. Greatness doesn't just endure because of that love. It thrives because of that love.

Section 5
Fairness and selfishness

It feels good to the self-centered mind to think in fairness, almost has the sound of righteousness, but the amount which is called fair is subjective and is declared so by an immature understanding of life. It came from judgments prone to lead to self-pity. Why do I have to have an equal amount of something that someone else has to be happy?

Is it fair to be the one who always loves first? Is the one who loves more the one who is the weakest? Is the one who loves more the most vulnerable? Absolutely not! It is the strongest who lead with love. It is the strongest that make the right choices when many others would veer from that path to obtain revenge, hate, or jealousy. To lead is to live true concepts first. It sets an example and chooses kindly to encourage others. It is strong that give back kindness when spoken harshly to. It is magnanimous who treat others back with high regard after being belittled. These are they who change the world, and though it isn't fair, it is love.

Love comes from being true to who we are
It is better to give than receive
It is better to love than be loved
It is better to be trustworthy than to be trusted
It is better to apologize than to be forgiven
It is better to forgive than to be apologized to
It is better to give respect than to be admired
Love is what we give because we care.

There is no real reference point or amount that determines what a fair share is. Those who complain often have this motive. This kind of thinking begins a war of back and forth posturing because we perceive differently what our fair share is. We feel hurt and shorted.

We can either be motivated by fairness or by love, but never both. They are opposites in their nature. We are doing service for someone because we care for them, not because we are trying to reach some kind of balance of good deeds with each other. When we want fairness we never seem to be satisfied. Equal shares of anything never brings a contentment with life but "pure motives" to love does.

As the angst of pity and self-righteous indignation grows inside us we feel entitled to make it fair. Fairness leads to the mass disrespect we call social justice, a justice that puts a group's privileges before the freedom of the individual.

If a fair world could exist, one without those who are destitute or treated unjustly, it would be a place where compassion isn't needed or learned, and strong character never developed. A place where greatness is never fashioned. We would be as though we had no arms, driven to get a fair share but nothing to hold it. We would have no appreciation for what we had.

We can believe the world should fair to everyone, and be disappointed, or we can believe the world needs love. We can experience this love bringing purpose, building good character, and bringing joy and peace.

Looking for a partner who will choose to love you starts with finding a partner who will love with you

Because life isn't fair, we have even a greater need to look for partners who can love.

Love's paradigm doesn't create a roseate view of things but rather one of hope. Both partners who love allow for mistakes, suffering, and challenges. It is a hope that pulls us back up again and again, only this time stronger, and more understanding. It provides reasons to live more conscientiously and more purposefully. What an amazing person one is, who first thought is, "How do I build hope?"

In everything we do together, we can do it for a loving reason. We can do it with a more loving effort. There is always a loving reason to do the right thing and that in itself is sufficient reason.

Section 6
Motives of choice

The constant want to love and cherish more makes it work

If a profound love is to come to our souls, it won't be because we accidentally fell in love. Those that see love in this way will constantly judge whether or not they are still in love and keep checking their feelings. They tie the word love to emotion instead of a virtue. The loving feeling is mystical and out of their power. Couples often marry because they fall in love and divorce because they fall out of love. The ironic thing is that believing it is a virtue with its correct definition, brings choices that allow for the loving feeling to be more constant and stronger in their lives. Love is not something to be earned or withheld.

Love it isn't something to be given when or because I feel it.
Love is not to be shared because I want it in return.
Love is given, or I choose to act because I care about others and want their happiness.
Love is given even when I am in a bad mood, upset or sad.
Love is given to others even when I am in physical pain or stress.
Love is given to someone, even if he or she has more things than I do, more free time than I do or more health than I do.

Wanting to love more has direction and motivation, a hope for a better future. Wanting to love more implies and inspires creativity as a part of the answer. When we decide to take someone else's life into our world the greatest gift we can give them is to value them more, and love and care for them more, every day.

Falling in love is nature's way of giving us a taste of the euphoria that is possible in marriage if we are respectful and do the work of love. Just the taste of this euphoria plants the seeds of hope. This euphoria is frequent and often in the lifetime of two people that make it happen. They can build strong bonds from their constant desire to cherish and care even "more" for the happiness of the other than they did yesterday. In taking this worthwhile challenge, they will create romantic memories and develop a deep appreciation for each other. They will cry with each other over tragedies and cheer each other in their triumphs.

Self-esteem is a concern that leaves the path of love

As esteem became the mind meme that gained greater control over our choices, being cool, fashionable and popular replaced our ability to articulate why something is aesthetic, of worth, or of character. Gang members are often tested and found to have high self-esteem no matter how devastating their lives are on those around them. Of what service was their high-regard? How much love did high self-esteem give? If asked, “Who do you think you are?” they may respond, “Cool,” or maybe, “Badass.” We as a society, in general, have stopped appreciating things for their intrinsic worth, even worse we value things for the prestige of those we want to impress. There is no reason to think rationally and then elucidate points that are relevant when things are valued based on prestige.

Those whose motives are to be esteemed will give up on love when it takes that they character. It’s easy to judge those we live with and rub elbows with, but until we can love those in which it takes real character and understanding- our cool rapport and superficial kudos with everyone else in the world is just an act.

Considering motives and rational thinking

What our hopes are centered around is what we are motivated by, and this determines the kind of thinking that validates and justifies it. The center of our hopes is the paradigm by which we view the world. Rational thinking is attained and practiced in the reasoning motivated by our true understanding of love, as well as respect for "who we are." When any motive is considered, other than respect and love, it takes from the purity of our motives. It takes from what should be the genuine concerns of our humanity.

-Love-

A feeling, a fullness, an adoration so endearing
And words there are none that can impart
The sublime emotion tugging at our hearts
Only a cherished glimpse, a taste of its virtue
To linger as evidence, that we need never part
Regardless of the challenge, of time, or of distance

Levels of motive or thinking

I'll give a simplistic view of four levels of thinking or motive below, using sharing and challenge as examples. Any hope we have and put central in our lives would also motivate our choices and determine what we believe is rational and truthful. These four different hopes are put in order, from the most irrational to rational.

1) What is in it for me?

These people do not share for they are simply looking out for themselves. Their desires and expectations are centered on achieving complacency, and being indulged, at any cost. It must profit them and make them look good. It must bend around their time and agenda. These people may have some inclinations for fairness. They think, "Is there enough in this for me to be worth the challenge it poses?" Many who think like this are prone to develop the vice of self-righteousness if this is what they want others to see. Many are motivated by a hope to be seen as righteous, fair, tough, or cool. In today's world, many do things for their self-esteem, to be seen as fair, or as cool.

2) Fairness

These people hope to make all things equal for everyone. Their idea of sharing is to make things equal by taking from some, who have more than most, to give to others that have less. They usually lack emotional intelligence and are stuck in a juvenile way of thinking. They have some propensity for what's in it for me and right and wrong. These often believe the greater the challenge it poses, the greater the unfairness there must be. Unfairness to them means others must be at fault.

These often believe that those who have it easier must have had privileges to get what they have. To these people, the ends of fairness justify the means of disrespect.

3) Right and wrong

These hope that doing the right thing (according to their definition of righteousness) will bring happiness. These people share because it's the right thing to do. They have some propensity for fairness and potential. They often feel guilty because it was wrong instead of feeling compassion for someone whose rights were disrespected. These see their challenges as tests of character. For them, this is a way to measure their righteousness.

4) Potential or love

These put their hopes in the fruits of our humanity. These share when it helps others in their well-being and potential, but holds back, if it doesn't. When this level is embedded in the soul, love is neither a reward nor something to be paid back. But instead, love is the way of living for the worth and well-being of others. If they progress, they will slowly lose the need to pat themselves on the back for their good deeds. They will find their satisfaction in the happiness of others and in learning.

These see challenges as opportunities to creatively find answers with love. In their minds, they haven't sacrificed anything. They haven't been treated unfairly. They are just taking the better path.

Section 7
Hard love (The difference in empathy and love)

While we learn to deal with anxiety, as we overcome our fears, we can spend some time learning and pass our time in admirable causes. Love is given in constant efforts whether life is a breeze or a battlefield. It is not concerned about how difficult the choice is, only if the choice must be made.

When there is a conflict between easing someone's pain or showing others how to ease their own pain, love chooses to allow them to do their own work. It is a practice everyone needs, better caring for one' happiness. "Caring for" someone's happiness (love), whether it is to love the self or others, is not the same thing as "feeling with" someone's happiness (empathy). Empathy is a receptive experience. It has no hopes, expectations, or agendas. Empathy is moved to end suffering, even when suffering is necessary. Love picks the course with the most human potential and happiness in the course of our "entire story."

Love, which is more akin to wisdom than it is to compassion, is hoping to help someone improve their gifts of humanity and find happiness through self-actualization. Hard love is brave, facing the hard truths and painful consequences and then moving forward in spite of it all. It does so with patience, without complaint, and without recognition.

Empathy wants to end hunger by handing out free fish. Love wants to educate, help people find jobs, and then find a sell on fishing polls. Love is brave enough to do whatever is necessary, even when it means leaving our comfort zones.

When a teenage boy acts up and gets in trouble, an empathetic mother may feel his guilt, frustration, and pains. She may even react to his feelings and pardon his indiscretion. A wise, loving father may care about his future happiness. He desires that his son take accountability for his actions and become a responsible person. Compassion doesn't always lead to wise decisions.

Though compassion is felt with empathy, its compassion must remain passive. Love must remain the motive of choice. Its kindness isn't generous to the point of crippling the potential and well-being of anyone. All principles of hope have an anticipation of future implications- even if it is to best to live the rest of today as content as we can and then plan for even better tomorrow's.

Empathy is not entirely software but the part of our mind that deeply feels with others does not even begin to develop till we reach about our eighteenth year of age. And the efforts to imprint empathetic pathways in our minds is still up to our choices, choices that bring a humble self-knowledge and engrained listening skills.

<u>The importance of fully giving empathy and love</u>

Loving intentions and choices may not always have enough impact on someone to influence them to change as powerfully as empathy will. The encounter of truly being understood and being accepted is a powerfully motivating experience. Love and real empathy are developed, for the greater part, independently from each other. Love is developed through a hope for others and empathy is developed through humility and the acceptance of others. Both experiences must be fully experienced.

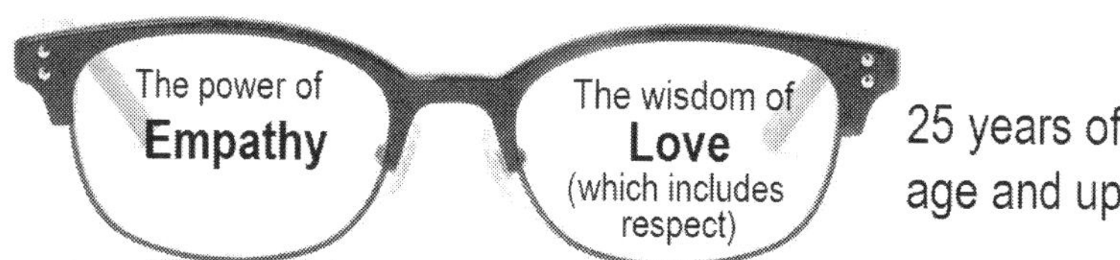

Tougher choices are needed when my boundaries are being crossed. And tougher choices are also needed when we are dealing with those that we have personal stewardship, such as our children or employees. We may have to say, "You're fired." "You will have to move out because you are abusing me." "You are on restriction." However, empathy is first shown, and then hard choices are made. Finally, a reminder is given to them that we do care for them.

<u>Self-Love</u>

Self-love begins with accepting those things about ourselves we cannot change, like, "I'm too short" "I have a weird smile"... When we do not accept those things about ourselves we cannot change we feel betrayed by ourselves. Interestingly enough what makes things most marketable are their unique qualities. If we can't love ourselves the way we are, how can we expect to love others the way they are? If you would hope that your child could accept themselves, forgive themselves, or hold themselves up with greater worth, why not do these for yourselves. Maybe they will learn from your example?

Self-Love is the ultimate effort to be responsible for one's own success, well-being, potential, and happiness.

Self-Love is characterized by a lack of blame on others for our lack of happiness within ourselves. We do not blame others for our unhappiness because of their lack of listening, or their lack of empathy. Our greatest friend needs to be the one who we can rely most on…and that is ourselves.

Self-Love is characterized as a person who puts faith in truth, finds happiness in hard times, and is kind to a fault. A person whose hope and self-encouragement are bigger than their challenges. It is someone who knows not self-pity. One who is not concerned about the fairness of life, but is interested in the opportunity love has to make a difference. One whose wants are merely passing thoughts but whose desire to care for human needs fuels their hopes for both the self and others.

Section 2
Building our Humanity

Now that the blueprints are clear it is time to build the house. Objectivity and creativity are far more essential to the potential and happiness of our humanity than they have been given credit for; and few texts, if any, have presented them in the light they deserve. The motives acted upon to respect and love turn into the substance of true greatness. Little by little the path true to "who we are" builds creativity, patience, listening skills, emotional skills, bravery, confidence, wisdom, etc.

The emotional intelligence we gain will aid in the house we build, to make it a home that we find peace and comfort in, and take satisfaction in. You will not find a better way of understanding our emotions and using them in practical ways to grow and be strong than in this book.

Chapter 5- Imagination & Creativity

An innocence is staring back at me
A world of pure imagination un-rushed
An innate love untainted and full of trust
A love that reaches in and lingers quietly
Where my own inner child hides from me
Disillusioned, and longing to be free.

Section 1
Imagination- evolving our possibilities

"Imagination is more important than knowledge. For knowledge is limited, whereas imagination embraces the entire world, stimulating progress, giving birth to evolution." -Albert Einstein. Imagination is the central faculty of what makes us humans and the substance of agency. When we imagine something good can be we hope. Imagination is what gives us such tremendous potential. With a healthy imagination and just a little faith just about anything is possible.

<u>Imagination plans the course of our lives</u>

Imagination inspires planning, it gives rise to proactive faith. We can imagine our relationships being beautiful and rewarding, and we can imagine doing things to make them this way. If we imagine the possibilities for this weekend's date, then we could plan for it.

A self-fulfilling prophecy is when what we imagine will happen, does. If our attitude says it's going to be a bad day, it probably will. Not because there weren't other possibilities but because our vision was too narrow. For, our life's path follows what we imagine will be the case. To live well we simply need to imagine well by imagining more worthwhile possibilities, to use our imagination for hope, faith, and charity. Imagination gives our agency more choices.

<u>The constant duplicity and opposing forces of our imagination</u>

Imagination is the parent and hope, trust, doubt, fear, and pride. This is how our agency plots its course to different harbors. Like children imagining in their minds the star character, and its monsters and battles to fight. We too in our minds have an imagination that fights itself. We plan to succeed and plan to fail at the same time and hardly notice. We often entertain thoughts and fed the desires that sabotage our lives. We strive to work for a singular mind, one that the sum of its imaginations synergize our success.

This duplicitous nature of our imagination requires us to let go of counterproductive thoughts and build healthy desires and attractions. So many choices are about slowly carving our singular character to a better world to enjoy. They require us to let go of something that can only give temporary pleasure today and sorrow tomorrow, for something that we know will bring more lasting success and happiness for the rest of our lives. Those who can quit smoking for better health, and those that can get better grades instead of partying so they can get into college, are exercising faith in all the future good they can imagine.

Things that blind the possibilities of our imagination

When we expect something will be the case we limit our imagination to the future possibility of only one scenario. This is a fault of using no objectivity. A dilemma is to imagine there are only two possibilities and usually one is at the expense of the other, like my way and your way when there are just many ways.

The reactionary imagination that causes fear, pride, or doubt is also the imagination that entertains them, causes them to grow, until they seem insurmountable. For example, we might expect something bad will happen and cause us to fear and then excessively fixate the fear. Expectations, fear, pride, doubt are horrible ruts that constantly deepen and become harder to escape the more we entertain them.

The worst kind is expectations is to believe, that for the other person's own good, it "better be" the case. Here our imagination poisons us and creates callous and mean people. Here we are implying if I do not get what I expect there will be hell to pay for someone else. This is an unfolding story no one wants to be a part of.

"Let no way be the way. Let no limitation be the limitation."

- Bruce Lee

<u>Hope is to imagine a better future,</u>

Whether it is seconds from now from a better attitude, or five years later from now, because of better education, hope imagines a better future and faith acts on it.

The best use of our imaginations is to imagine that something good "can" be the case, whether it's by the next step we take or from much planning and many interim goals. This kind of positive imagination just might be our best friend, especially if that imagination is choreographed and imbued from the mind of love.

<u>Hopeful imagination is open to new possibilities and new challenges</u>

Hope is to imagine and believe in a better tomorrow but implies I have to make it that way. A love based hope knows that whatever "is" the case, hope will stick around till the purposes of love are accomplished. It will not be disappointed, discouraged, or give up, for an imperfect world is a part of Life's story; an imperfect world is a part of every love story. Hope is the most fundamental and distinguishing characteristic of love. Its hope is never-ending. And though I do not have the results, or even answers now, with continued imagination and creativity, I will. Hope is objective to anything new to either help achieve our dream or achieve something else entirely better.

Hope is:

An assurance we "have" when we anticipate a favorable future. This assurance remains alive by believing if not this answer then there will be another. If not at this time then it will happen later.

Hope based in loving motive says, "no matter what happens, we will still make the best of life and enjoy what is- while new plans are being made." Hope is also open to the fact there may be other things as desirable or even more desirable. Though life is always an unfolding process, and there are often unexpected turns, but hope and love remain open, positive, pleasantly patient, and ever kind.

The seed of faith is nourished in hope, the tender sprout grows to become strong and patient. With constant positive imagination and faithful choice, hope grows deeper roots and feeds a vibrant tree. Patience with life, self, and others turns to kindness and love- a love that fills us with joy. The kind branches allow for the birds to rest and nest, and to be safe from predators.

Figure 4

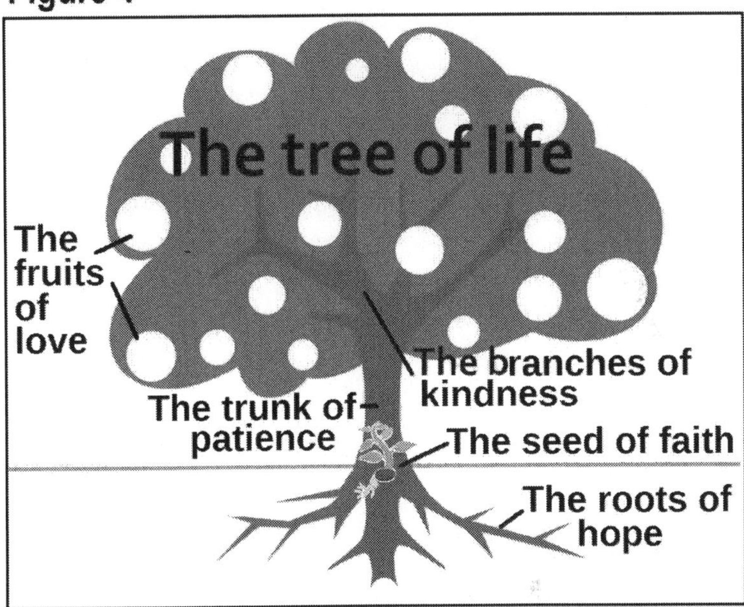

Section 2
Two congruous paths of healthy Imaginings

One study of centennials concluded the only factor that they have in common was there positive outlook on life itself. "Dr. Nil Barzilai, a study co-author and director of the Albert Einstein College of Medicine's Institute for Aging Research." Another study at Stanford University, published Feb 15th strongly correlates better brain activity with a positive attitude.

I have found that the centennials sharing their stories with me had this positive mind. They always imagined good things were around the corner, they had bright hopes all their lives. And the people they knew were important (if only in their eyes).

A healthy imagination start in an imperfect world

Hopefully, we too will use our imagination to serve us well. But we can veer too far in our imaginations to the real world of humans that all struggle with their humanity. For instance, those that imagine they will find the right person that will "make" them happy, these might as well imagine them wearing a cape that has a big red S on it. Our imagination should leave the unicorns in the cartoons, and the Superman cape in the comics, and out of our choices.

Our imagination can best serve us aimed at real human beings that will make mistakes at times. We need an imagination that sees apologies and forgiveness, and other true precepts, as a means to get us there. Our imagination must include that we must set boundaries at times and reinstate our goals. When we imagine our true love- we should imagine that this person, like the rest of the planet, will also make mistakes. We must also leave room for the certainty that this person will have made mistakes.

The intra-congruous imagination- Creating worthwhile things for a better tomorrow

Like all gifts, the more we proactively use our imagination the better we become at using it as an effective tool. Sometimes the only gifted imagination we enjoy is from the imagination of a few who entertain us. Sadly, we allow ourselves to be entertained to overshadow our boredom, a boredom caused by the neglecting of our imagination in the first place. In our modern world of titillating things and conveniences, that help us skirt by, our imaginations are rusty and inept. It is more and more left on the constant reactionary mode, of fear, pride, and doubt.

Creativity is knowledge, skill, and imagination in play together

All things created were first imagined in our minds. We must imagine the smaller steps, the supportive goals. Finally, I need to view the difficulties I am sure will come across as challenges rather than obstacles. We can imagine the obstacles we will cross, and how we will deal kindly with them, and then finally create something new, beautiful and amazing.

In all of our imaginings there is a place for doubt.
Doubt your doubts.
Doubt your pride.

Illustration 7 : 5 paths of imagination

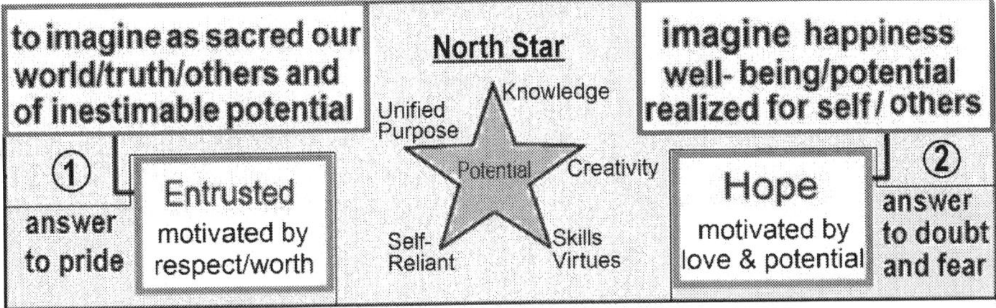

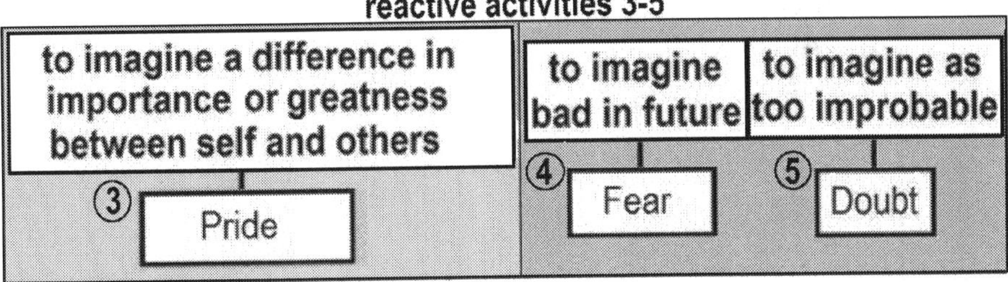

This illustration breaks our imagination down into five categories of imagination. The first two have fidelity and utility to who we are, the North Star. The other three lead us in paths away from our potential.

Imagination and creativity are not child's play, they are the most productive use of our time when done with the right purpose.

Can you just imagine the effects of having an imagination that gravitates towards and dwells heavily on these three things?

1) Imagining those we share our world as of great worth,

2) Imagining our world as of great worth and opportunity,

3) Imagining our lives spent creatively blessing others with happiness and well-being.

We tend to think of creativity as an artistic gift, but its greatest contribution is in the everyday miracles that renew life and feed the soul with joy and satisfaction. The desire to love more changes our outlook unlocks creativity and brings out our best.

Believing is seeing. It is the sustenance of creation.

-I imagine I can-
Though I stand on the ground I look to the sky-
To reach that pinnacle my mind says might.
Is it so unbelievable, is my dream too high?
Why not take heart in what feels so right?
For vision is more than just seen with the eye
I think with my gift to imagine I should fly.

Section 3
Eleven tips for imagination and creativity

<u>1) Commit to proactively use our imagination and be creative</u>

Make the commitment that creativity will be practiced and used to enjoy life and that it will be used to find the answers to the challenges in life. We must always use our imagination projected through the lenses of love and respect. An imagination that sees the potential me. One that transforms who I am. One that finds various creative ways to both expresses ourselves, our options, and our love.

<u>2) Keep a journal and practice the details in our story</u>

"What is it I want to create?" Write it down! Look at this every day. Imagine it happening with creativity and love. Be specific. "I'm hoping to pass the bar next month and join Uncle Charles in his law practice." Specific language keeps in mind correlation and relevance. "I'm hoping that we find more intimacy and joy in our relationship and that each one of us feels more appreciated." This is better than saying, "I am hoping our relationship lasts or that it is good." We would see that the more details we can bring up and imagine the more alive and productive our hope becomes.

<u>3) Know our worth</u>

Our ability to learn, create, and make a difference is unimaginable. We should never say, "I can't," but, "It might take some time." Faith in our potential leads to patience in ourselves. We will eventually reap the rewards of living principles of truth. Never give up. We are capable. Trust that our creativity will grow. As long as we don't give up, we will succeed. We can express daily in grand affirmation, "You and I are of illimitable worth, and unfathomable potential." "Anything is possible if I can imagine it."

<u>4) Create an alert, open, and positive mood, attitude, and environment</u>

Just by making the effort to imagine new possibilities we become open to those possibilities. To believe is the first step in making things happen.

When tired some can take a five-minute power nap is all it takes to be alert. I find when I am too tired to think I start a project with something I can do that doesn't take much thought and I soon find myself lost in the work and more alert.

If our mood is a little low, we can put on some good music. Catch your words of doubt, fear, and negativity and then think of things in a more positive light. Use affirmations that direct imagination and inspire us. We can creatively make affirmations that are tailored to our challenges and needs. How many positive affirmations can you write down about something worthwhile you want? "This is worth my every effort." "This is going to be a great and productive day."

<u>5) Enjoy and feel the emotional rewards of Creativity, and bring emotional rewards to others</u>

Creativity is a gift of humanity and with each step that we make in our potential, comes the feelings of joy, satisfaction, contentment, delight, and peace. Smell the roses, live in the moment, and find the joy that is waiting to be felt. Recognize the positive emotions that flow as we creatively connect with others, find answers, and accomplish a new task. Enjoy the path that leads to the goals.

Take time to celebrate progress. Take time to thank others for their help, find the good in others.

6) Gain knowledge

In every role that we play and each goal we strive for, we should seek a deeper understanding. With every hope, we wish to make true, learn everything we can about it. Learning itself helps us see things in new ways and put new things into practice. We can get information from those who are successful at what you want to do. Look up professional opinions and find studies on the internet. Find those successful in what you are hoping for and ask them how they achieved what they have. We can learn vocabulary that helps us express ourselves better or gain knowledge and skills that relate to our goals. Knowledge gives us options for creativity to be put to work. Remember invention is just taking existing truths and finding new ways to connect them.

7) Brainstorm and explore our curiosity and imagination

What other things could affect the outcome? What other perspectives could one have? What might happen, if I introduce something new? We can find questions that relate to our skill, vocation, relationship, goals. We can record any inspiration we get as soon as we can.

8) Brake our ultimate goals down to smaller goals

We can break the large goals into several smaller goals that are easier to obtain. Our large goals often seem too impossible to achieve. Imagination serves us best when it is aimed at things that are close in reach. Our imagination is more vivid for those things that are more attainable. Imagine the step that is just in front of you, and when that is reached, then imagine the next step.

9) Every day, in everything we do, is a time for creativity

There is an opportunity for creativity in everything we do in life. Any time is time to be creative. We are the artist and life is our canvass. It is a way to bring life to the moment and break free of the ruts we get stuck in. Even when we are having a hard time falling to sleep, imagine lying on a hammock, on a peaceful and vacant beach, the warm sun on your face, a light breeze on my skin, and the gentle swing of the hammock. Hear the ocean waves in the background. Using imagination as something we control and use for our good can be a habit. Creativity is a close friend we take with us everywhere we go like finding ways to breach conversations to strangers in the grocery store lines, at the doctor's office or the familiar surroundings of home.

10) Take risk

No one is completely sure what tomorrow brings. One thing is for certain we gain nothing when we do not try. Creativity is a part of that faith exercised that says I'll get started, even if I can't see the way right now, and I'll figure it out as I move forward. At worst, we learned something didn't work, and we can try in a better way.

11) Develop objectivity, think for myself

Objectivity pulls us from the insanity of group thinking, and the unhealthy beliefs society deems as normal. We need to truly listen to every opinion, imagine perspectives that haven't even been presented. Question everything we are told to believe. What is the probability that something is true, and what else might be true or useful?

Chapter 6- Faith and Objectivity

Which is more real and which more surreal
Is it of sleeping or waking?
And though my night's dreams are bazaar,
It is at day, I swing at ghost afar.
For all my hopes and dreams awaking,
Vanish by the nightmares of my making.

Section 1
Objectivity-keeping it real

We have heard that men are from Mars and women from Venus-but when it comes to our beliefs, we are all from different planets. Everybody is unique. We are from different families, religions, cultures, and life experiences. Each individual has a different fingerprint and a different personality.

If you want to understand people don't read books that put people into categories, learn objectivity, listening skills, humility and empathy and you will not only understand the people in your life they will also feel understood.

As she leaves for her first day of high school her freshman year, her father pleads her to pick good friends. Her reply, "Dad you are too judgmental." When she got home, he asked what friends she made. She said, "I found six Gothic friends." Her dad replied, "Out of two thousand students of different nationalities, colors, religions, and interest you found only those dressed in Gothic clothes are good friends. Who is judgmental?" She later told her dad trying to be the most Gothic was a way to compete and feel good about herself. For those who rely on esteem instead of self-worth getting out of the best of friends can be difficult.

Objectivity remains open primarily to further learn the truth value of things that seem reasonable or the probability of things pertinent to our lives. For, there isn't enough time to have too many misplaced hopes in cure-all remedies, tarot cards, horoscopes, men are from Mars, color personalities, or different ways we feel loved. Do we believe that giving gifts, in and of itself, is a way to bring others to their potential or real happiness? The daughter could have just as well looked for yellow personalities to have as friends and missed the best one she could have ever had.

It is the mark of an educated mind to entertain
a thought without accepting it. -Aristotle

A greater look into objectivity

Objectivity is the most fundamental virtue and is inclined to:

A) Trust my physical senses with each experience, so that I can come to rely on what is real in my external world. Objectivity holds one's own personal experience of their world as being the most valuable.

B) Imagine there is more in life to learn and experience than what I have personally experienced so far.

C) Receive second-hand information as "possible" truths when given with sound reason. It also receives other eye witnessed accounts, as "possibly" true. Objectivity is not the effort to discover the definitive truth, rather it is open to discovering more facts in an unfolding story.

Honesty is:

A) To be objective in category one of truth (the natural sciences). It is the "intention and efforts" to express what I have experienced or perceive to be the case, without exaggerations, embellishments, minimizing, normalizing, or rationalizing.

B). In category two (conceptual truth) includes the "intention" of developing and living from the pure motive of respect. "I did what I believed is considerate of everyone."

In category two, because the truth is determined by the fact it does not cross the boundaries of our potential or rights, it follows, for example, bullying would be dishonest behavior.

Section 2
Objectivity a fundamental virtue

Objectivity is the most fundamental in the virtues of entrustment. Without objectivity, there is no humility, empathy, or respect. Without objectivity, our faith would often discourage us. Objectivity is like a recording device which is always meant to be left on. It leaves our minds always ready for added understanding.

Subjectivity limits ourselves to the walls within our minds it uses an imagination that limits the human possibilities of all that can be.

Subjective is:
A) "A perceived reality" in our minds that is understood through false beliefs. It is our imagination that creates fear, doubt, and pride.
B) To "react" or be subject to a perceived reality or to false beliefs.
C) All "internal processes" of perceiving and of motive such as thought, emotion, desire, attractions, moods, inclinations, instincts, affinities and so forth. But not the senses that record our external world: sight, touch, sound, hear, and smell.
D) The "inclination" to keep coming to judgments or conclusions.

The many advantages of an objective mind

Objectivity's lack of bias allows it to have an attitude of being impartial and inclusive. Objectivity's inability to blow things out of proportion keeps the events in our own lives in perspective and from succumbing to imaginary, irrational, and improbable fears.

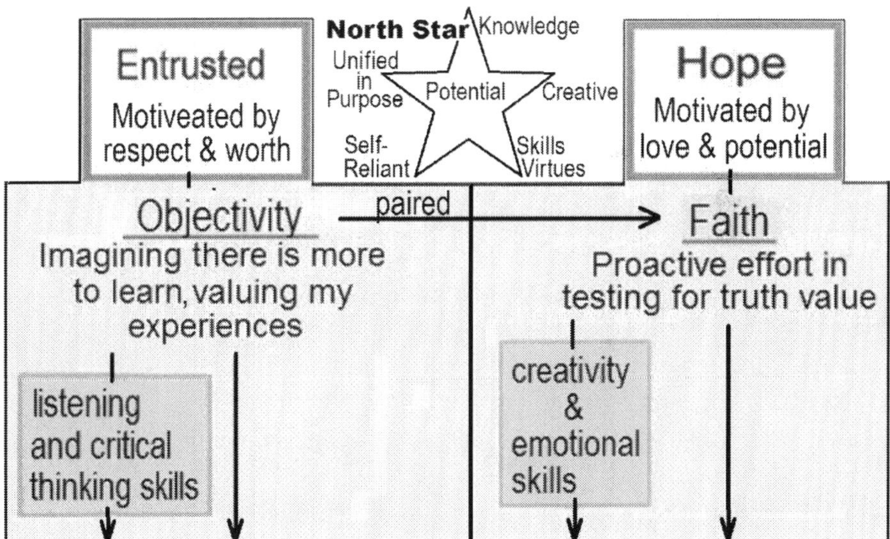

With objectivity, we trust our own senses and we are less gullible. When someone tells us that lemons are sweet, and we've tasted their sour nature, we know better. Objectivity accepts the details as they are "experienced' over those that are reported.

When we are open to the world around us we learn from a greater range of human experience.

Where objectivity is of being "open" to probable truths, faith is then the "testing" of those possible truths to see by my own experience and that they can be relied on to bring greater "quality" to life. Objectivity leaves you open to the unfolding stories of others. It gives you to have richer world of experience to draw from. Learning by faith is to verify that indeed a possible truth others have shared, or that you may have imagined to be possible, has relevance to success and happiness. It remains open, it is not conclusive, for there is always the possibility that something else can be more productive.

-Sons-
I knew you before you were here,
I loved you before you were near
I saw you & you touched my heart...
I loved you even more.
We laughed, we cried, we learned together…
I taught you and you taught me all that I lost,
The beautiful childlike love and faith…
We grew together...
And then you left to start a family of your own
Now you laugh, you cry with your son.
He teaches you & you teach him,
Now you know all you meant to me.

Section 3
Objectivity and faith

<u>The pairing of objectivity and faith</u>
Faith is:
A) A virtue in choosing to have a hope in the blessings that come from the admirable goals that my gifts are capable of.

B) It is to test "plausible" truths in hopes they will realize my potential, bring happiness, and reach my goals... (3rd law of logic) Antonym: Doubt.

To walk by faith is to continually face the light of hope and just take it a step at a time...ever brighter, higher, and evermore true to who you are.

As long as we are open to the possibility of success there is hope, not that it will happen but that it can. As long as it is possible there is hope. Faith, our proactive effort to try, and a hopeful imagination feed each other- trying more possibilities till we succeed. Each time we learn something new, we gain something new to exercise our faith in. Being objective aids to multiply our possibilities.

<u>Agency, imagination, objectivity, and the experiment of faith</u>

The human gift of our agency has dominance over any other genetic prepossessions toward choice. This axiom probably has the most profound application of anything else written in this book. It is so powerful that we could even choose to starve ourselves to death in the midst of plenty. We need to come to understand that we always have a choice. Agency also has dominance over any external forces egging and pushing us in every direction. With faith, our agency has incredible power. It also has dominance over internal forces; whether they are emotional, psychological or habitual tendencies. We don't have to do what we immediately think or feel. We can choose what we believe and what principles to trust and act upon. We can always take a break and imagine more possibilities.

Agency and the imagination that drives it is also dominant over every force that vies against us, to obstruct our potential from moving forward, because at its disposal are incredible concepts of success and happiness that we can choose to live by. Without this understanding, one could not exercise the faith needed to accomplish their most aspiring goals.

Probably the most insidious lie we tell ourselves is that the gifts we have, the concepts we can grasp, and the virtues we can develop are not enough to accomplish any personal or societal goal.

Objectivity is to doubt our doubts.

We may not know every step we need to take to achieve our goal, but getting started with faith is the hardest part. The harmonic virtue of faith is objectivity. We need to be objective enough to be able to look to modify or change our beliefs and plans when they prove unsuccessful. Faith always includes “But if not now, or soon, I will figure it out"- Faith has to be flexible enough to learn and try in a new way if needed.

<u>As adults, we have become attached to our beliefs</u>

To some degree being “attached” to our beliefs is a good thing. This is not the same thing as being opinionated which is one who thinks his beliefs are unassailable facts. To be opinionated is to believe that what we have not experienced or witnessed ourselves is true. Be in the habit of saying the affirmation, “But I could be wrong.”

Objectivity is to doubt our pride.

Holding on to our beliefs is healthy, not that our beliefs are right, rather it is that we are not easily fooled. What we believe in should come from the convictions within us, and that has come with some personal pondering and a preponderance of the evidence. Our beliefs should be held tightly and only changed with much thought. When the clever car salesman makes his emotional appeal, or the demagogue paints an ugly picture of things to fear and bring despair and then promises the answers. We should already stand on some solid ground. When peer pressure nags us to give in, those beliefs we hold on to inside keep us tethered and true to the self.

Objectivity doesn't mean we are so openly gullible as to become a chameleon, changing with every new opinion set before us. It just means we are open to listen to other's opinions and to hear other witnesses that seem to be "possible" truths. It doesn't throw away beliefs that faith has trusted in and that has been helpful, but it is open to the possibility there is more or that something could work better, especially when presented with a strong argument.

Section 4
Listening an exercise in objectivity

When we listen we ask questions to verify what we heard, we repeat what was said and how we understood it, and then ask, "Is this what you really mean?" We learn to take interest in the stories of others and ask questions that clarify and allow the other to be better understood. "What else happened?" "Anything else you want to tell me about?" "How did that make you feel?" "Why might you have felt that way?" Objectivity is always interested in the unfolding story.

Communication is two people taking more complete turns telling their stories and being understood, instead of the back and forth abrupt arguments of wills and trying to prove one is right. In objective listening, where each has fully been listened to, seeds are planted and respect is given. Each is freely allowed to express themselves and go on their merry way. Each has been transformed by intimacy. No one has to win an argument but they should at least have been given the chance to fully give and explain their beliefs. Each is given something to ponder on their own.

Many with sound beliefs haven't learned to logically support them. Perhaps their beliefs were handed to them by mentors that studied and pondered. While many, with irrational beliefs, have an abundance of "facts" and reasons handed to them by educators. Many of which studied through their lives with closed minds to prove an ideology they wanted to believe in. A theory that fits immoral and disrespectful lifestyles. Their lacking of objectivity has kept them from discovering and testing other theories. We would be unwise to let go of what we know has actually brought us happiness because others argue well.

Section 5
Faith is not in magic

In essence, each choice to get up and do something is an act of faith that something is true. Like getting up to flip the light switch on. We don't know it will go on, but we also know it won't magically go on. The bulb may be broken. It's the thought of believing it works and the act of getting up and flipping the switch that makes it faith. If the light doesn't go on, faith assumes something understandable is the cause, and faith becomes the power to find out why. The faith to move a mountain is the faith that it can be moved with the right effort, based on true principles, and with enough time.

There is no such thing as faith without believing that there will also be true cause and effect, the 3rd law of logic. We won't magically become doctors

Faith is not high self-esteem nor self-confidence

Today's teens score higher in self-confidence than the generation past but score lower in math tests. Article on 7-5-2013 called, "HIGH CONFIDENCE NOT TRANSLATING TO HIGH MATH SCORES FOR AMERICAN AND EUROPEAN STUDENTS" –Dr. Nima Sanandaji.

The doctrine of self-esteem is appealing. It allows for certain arrogance and disconnects from our common humanity. It is not efficacious towards our worthy goals because it misses the mark. Many call high self-esteem confidence in the self. They argue that this confidence makes us successful and happy, but this tenet has the cart before the horse. Knowledge of the truth, validating the truth by our actions, and enjoying the positive consequences of that choice- brings a person confidence in the gifts of humanity and confidence in true principles.

Can confidence in ourselves reach a goal of which we are ignorant of the facts, or we are bereft of the needed skills to achieve it? Thinking that because I think highly of myself I will be successful is misplaced confidence. Having our hopes up for something we are incompetent in just leaves us more frustrated.

I remember my first dance recital, my lack of balance and my two left feet. I stumbled around and was humiliated. Even if nature gave me a confident gene, I lacked skill and polished grace. After a year of practice it all seemed more natural, and where my balance had failed me, now I felt as if I could float and my confidence grew.

The teaching of self-esteem is spiritual abuse

We need confidence in the gifts of our humanity, when developed, better answers our challenges. Once our minds stop pursuing the real path of "who we are," than any pursuit taking time or energy, even that of high self-esteem, will just take us farther from our potential. The act of judging ourselves creates doubt in our ability to develop our gifts. Anything open to judgment is also open to doubt. The principles that allowed me to become a better dancer were intangible but real- practicing my routines correctly and remaining determined.

The enabling of self-esteem by parents and teachers is perhaps the greatest abuse of our humanity in our modern world. It is spiritual abuse. It is a teaching that is counterproductive towards reaching potential and happiness. The more parents and teachers try to protect a child's self-esteem the more they inadvertently teach them to judge themselves as well as others. They will pick up the protection of their egos and they will begin to see themselves as fragile. It is a mismatched waste of psychological energy that will lead no doubt to more doubt.

The protection of self-esteem instills in the victim the beliefs they are insufficient. Words such as "It is OK you're just not good at math" the message the child gets is they are not capable, instead of you just haven't applied yourself long enough and in the rights ways yet. When teaching our children to quit, they will see themselves as deficient.

Judging becomes a habit. It may be that at first, they judge whether or not they feel good about themselves, whether they are capable, next whether they are happy, and then whether they are loved. The constant judging brings them misery, self-pity, and since life is not fair.

Life gave us challenges to overcome that by so doing we come to know and have confidence in truth as a friend and ally. They are principles that have real cause and effect regarding our common authentic potential and the happiness that flows from them.

We need to teach self-worth that leads to self-acceptance, and self-respect. It is a faith that leads to our patience with ourselves. Teach each child the equal worth of others which leads to the acceptance of others and the respect of others. This leads to our patience with others. Teach each child to put faith in truths that work for everyone. Don't give them room to question whether or not they can achieve what they want, only whether or not they will do what is necessary to achieve it. Their ability to achieve is not in question. Teach each child to grow in virtues like discipline, patience, hard work, and taking satisfaction in all that he or she does.

When I came to my mother with complaints she told me, "Be like a boat on the water, don't let the water get inside and sink you." She taught me to be strong.

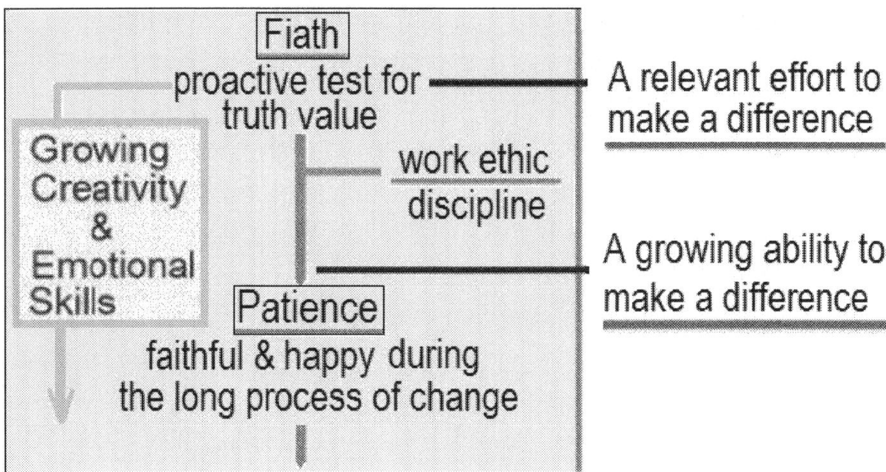

All of us from time to time will not feel good about ourselves, our lives, our spouses...etc. It is normal, it is human. Every kind of thought and emotions is coming our way, but these moments can be fewer and farther between for all of us. Our thoughts are never proof we have genetic tendencies for anything. Some of these thoughts are simple suggestions from a world of influences we may not even be aware of. Agency decides if the thoughts are valid, to rethink, reimagine, and to make new goals. It is time to stop the water from coming in and sinking me every time someone has a bad opinion of me, or if I have a distressing thought or mood. In real life, storms come and go, and so do emotions, moods, thoughts, beliefs, opinions, attractions...etc. I "my agency" am the captain of my soul and I decide the course of my life.

Section 6
Patience finding happiness in the journey

Patience, like all virtues of love and respect, is aimed at our humanity. It is to have hope, which is the set it belongs to, with the added quality to endure well. This ability to endure well builds greater character; one that keeps from quitting in our goals, and holds a frame of mind that leads us to be much kinder to the self and others.

Patience is:
A) Faith through an unfolding story, that our potential will unfold as it should with continued effort and time.
When paired with humility, comparing our choices to who we are, our North Star will remain before us: a fixed motive of hope, reminding us of our worth and showing us the direction to steer the ship.
B) Remaining hopeful, through an unfolding story, because of the belief and effort that the greater good is best achieved through love and respect- especially through time.
When paired with empathy patience for others is easier to exercise.
C) Patience has at it heart the emotional skill of resilience and finds satisfaction and appreciation during an unfolding process, regardless of its challenge.

Patience is also the ability to enjoy our time while we wait, putting things in order and preparing for the day our blessing comes.

Our challenges never become easier- with sustained hope and faith we just become stronger, happier, and kinder in spite of them. While impatience is the unwillingness to be happy, or put faith in truth or virtue, over the necessary length of time to realize our goal.

Many people attribute patience with suffering. They think that if they endure poorly, whining till they get what they want, they have been exercising patience. All the while, their impatience had the added bonus of showing everyone else just how unfair or hard life is for them. They lack the "emotional resilience" (covered in the 8th chapter) needed to allow others the courtesy of enjoying their day. Enduring impatiently for what we are hoping for isn't patience. It is disrespectful to those we live with. Virtues that we hold to do not leave the foul taste of constant complaining in the air.

A tool for being patient "H.A.P.P.Y."

H) Is for a hope that imagines a bright future.

A) Is for affirmations that get me through and lift my spirit. "I will get through this" "This is a normal challenge in life that helps me grow in character." "We are all imperfect, we all make mistakes, but we will grow and do better." "From time to time we all feel emotional pain but we get through it."

P) Is for positive and happy. "Everything is going to turn out alright' I will do things that bring me joy and satisfaction in life while I wait for my goals.

P) Is for proactive. Patience is the birthing place of love, a proactive virtue. It is time to show what love can do. I must make my blessing happen instead of waiting for them to come to me.

Y) Is for yes I can. Yes, I can cope with this. Yes, I can calm my anxieties. Yes, and I can calm my emotions and create space to think from other points of view. Yes, I can be grateful for what I have, and I will find joy through others and their successes.

Chapter 7- Emotions
Road Signs of Our Humanity

A feeling, a fullness, an adoration endearing
And words there are none that can impart
The sublime emotion tugging at my heart
Only a cherished glimpse, a taste of its virtue
To linger as evidence that we never part
Regardless of challenge, of time, of distance

Section 1
The emotional challenge of a modern world

What is real for us isn't just what we see or hear, but what we feel in our hearts. Each experience we have is one that affects the whole soul. The emotional experience is what brings our world to life, gives life its depth, and is the very substance for which we live.

The concepts and virtues of bravery, compassion, hope, and sacrifice would not even be words in our vocabulary without emotions. Emotions help us understand, prioritize, and build character. They are the excitement of our challenges and the joy in our triumphs. With our emotions, we will feel our worth, feel empowered and confident in our abilities, and we feel the depth of our gratitude for our blessings.

Because technology came upon us like a sudden storm, we did not predict its impact on our humanity. We are unprepared for its effects on us personally. The easy life has made us emotionally inept. We need a new understanding and approach to emotional skills that can compensate for the effects of a facile and sedentary life. We are more impatient and anxious; and, on average, our emotions are seemingly more discordant and painful than ever before.

When we take in the whole picture, life's ups and downs, failures and triumphs- the contrast paints a striking picture of the wisdom of life and its amazing ride that forges beautiful souls.

Unfortunately, in today's world, emotional pain is unwelcome. It isn't that the things that caused the emotional pain are unwelcome but the emotions that cry out for us to change are. It would be nice for many to find happiness in false beliefs that promise the easy road. It would be nice to take a pill that gives everlasting energy without consequence. As we get better at the temporary avoidance of emotional pain, we become less tolerant of it. I say temporary for that is the best we will ever do. Our emotions will have their say.

Many have fallen to the temptation of covering the pain with drugs. But, the longer the drug is taken the more destructive it is on our health and the more behind we are in our maturational growth. Someday the chasm, between our lack of preparation in life and where we should be, will be too obvious for alcohol or any drug to hide.

If our lives were spent “enduring well,” through one hardship and challenge after another, then human beings would become extremely tenacious. If in life we answered our emotional pain's reasons for being we would live with an abundance of emotions that reflect better choices. Yes, trials themselves would still come, life is full of disasters; but we, without bending or yielding, would pass through the very jaws of hell- without flinching an eye and merrily singing as we go.

The emotional struggles that we endure “well” will be the refining fire of our life, and not merely our experiences.

Section 2
Emotions, the truth of our humanity

We hear all the time, “My heart says one thing and my mind another.” This is a dilemma caused by our misunderstanding of emotions and what they are saying to us. Just as our physical pains point to our mortality, our emotional pains point to our humanity. Our agency then can take these biological signals as information to be understood in the care of the soul. Feeling pain with a broken leg or feeling bad when we do bad things has practical and far-reaching importance. We need the motivation to care for ourselves. Even the word emotion means to be internally stirred up to action, and all emotions can become preludes to making wise choices if we understand them and manage them.

Emotions and our good sense are needed in cooperation- a dance, if you will, in a mature and creative mind. They are friends with different languages. Our agency sorts through their advice and wisely steers its course. It is the job of our agency to manage our thoughts and feelings, as though they are separate crew members with different skill sets. Each has its unique contributions that the soul needs.

Discordant emotions tell us that something is lost, disrespected, disconnected, neglected, or even "out of balance," when it comes to our unfolding potential. But for most of us, we simply react to our emotions instead of seeing them as a need to be more conscientious of our true needs. When we feel lonely we can choose to take care of ourselves. We can turn to our need for intimacy that helps us to connect, be understood and loved for who we are.

Anything else I do with my feelings other than taking charge of them, whether it's ignoring them, burying them, reacting to them, fearing them, embellishing them, punishing someone by them, seeking pity with them, finding someone to blame for them or panicking over them- will have detrimental effects on my life.

<u>Emotional pain reminds us that there is a work to do</u>

Physical pain is the consequences for our body's mistreatment or disrespect. This is because our physical potential is fixed to our biological truth. Our humanity is no different. Emotional pain exists because we violated conceptual truth, failed to apply fundamental principles that guide our humanity, failed to develop virtues, or have experienced a loss of someone we with whom shared a closeness.

Emotions are the road signs that show us our choices are connected to the truth of "who we are." As this gap grows, between where we are and where we should be, the discord emotions get more persistent and stronger.

The longer we ignore our North Star, the farther we drift off course.

Though the errata of our false beliefs and vain imaginations are not so lucidly up for our view, the emotions that live inside us are more candid. If we are on a voyage to find "who we are," then just listen to our hearts. The first contribution of discordant emotion is its ability to show us the truth of those trespasses, appetites, omissions, choices, and thoughts that disrespect who we are. Unlike our reasoning mind, which is causing us all our problems, our emotions don't have an agenda nor can they deceive.

The quickest way to change ourselves, in the artful use of our agency, is to take ownership of our thoughts and emotions and change how we relate to them. We need to see them as being useful tools to be used skillfully for our potential growth instead of fearing them or pitying ourselves because we have them. We need to learn how to use all of what we are and experience in a skillful way. Instead of the usual panic and fear because our emotions are painful... having a new way of dealing with emotions is a running start to emotional health.

Section 3
The emotions of happiness

<u>For humanity emotions are the reason it is a challenge</u>

For our humanity opposition is mostly found in our emotional struggles.

There is opposition to all things, whether macroscopic or microscopic, whether contrived by perfectly sound logic, or in practice in the physical world. The electron has its positron, the North Pole and the South Pole, empathy and apathy, happiness or misery, and choosing the high road or one without admirable goals. Opposites are parities that have no meaning without the other. The law of opposition for us is to choose to be faithful to "who we are" against opposing forces. Like lifting weight builds strength of body choosing the right against opposition builds strength of character. Our emotions reflect this world of opposites in intangible concepts fearful or hopeful, at peace or disturbed, lonely or connected, happy or miserable, overwhelmed or confident.

<u>The expanding of an emotional toolbox</u>

These primary faculties we feel as infants: trust, hope, and fear later attach to beliefs we adopt. The attachment of our primary faculties and primary feelings with concepts rise to more types of feelings and even virtues and vices.

Most feelings are a mixture of feelings, or feelings colored by judgment, as most in this list are a mixture of things. Like adding red to yellow we get orange. Emotions are the same way. To be horrified is to be surprised by fear, rage is to be surprised by anger, and delight to be surprised by other's personal accomplishments or surprised by a savory experience. Content is peace mixed with the belief the course of my life is an admirable one. Anger is frustration mixed with judgment.

We do not need to be trapped in a single emotion because we are capable of feeling many things at once. This understanding is vital in our ability to cope through hard times. We can change our attitude and appreciate what is also good even when we are sad, disappointed, or discouraged.

As we pass through our childhood, fundament emotions and faculties are mixed with other emotions, beliefs, moods, attitudes, and virtues. When it comes to our well-being, our choices, and happiness- it will not matter what we classify any of these, they can be still treated as emotions with the same skills. Our agency having the final say to all things subjective, like moods, attractions, and aptitudes, they all point to our universal humanity from which they came. They are either in discord to who we are or they are in harmony to who we are.

When we practice principles of truth we feel emotions like these: acceptance, of worth, joy, peace, satisfaction, contentment, confident and delight. Principles that bring happiness through time will become dear to us. We are moved to defend these principles and values. We are moved to share these as well. Finally as the motive to love others and give them reasons to be happy arises to the character to more fully do so. This service becomes less a burden to do and more a joy to be a part of. See illustration in Ch.4 section 1.

The five primary emotions of happiness- Mostly an effect from the proactive efforts of "hope"

Joy is to feel animated well-being (almost like an automatic inner "celebration of the value" of life.) It fills our soul in healthy activities with others and with "a step toward" our admirable goals in any of the five areas of our potential.

Content is a feeling of "being on the right course" when our unfolding story, is and has been in step with who we are.

Satisfaction is a feeling of "relief" when an admirable hope or goal is answered.

Delight is to be surprised by joy.

Peace is a feeling of inner "tranquility" from living in harmony with guiding principles that are congruous to who we are and with those that share our world.

The five primary emotions of happiness are the effect of approximation of our potential in the path of a proactive and love inspired hope. They are not the same as primary feelings like fear, hope, and abandonment. Joy is both a primary emotion and a primary emotion of happiness.

Secondary emotions of happiness- Mostly emotions of "worth"

Connected, complete, of worth/appreciated, comforted, confident, to appreciate, relief, accepted, an admiration for, revere/reverent, awe…Except for confident, these are emotions of worth that lie the path of respect. A few of them mix with and are a part of the primary emotions.

Teaching our children to proactively create an emotionally rewarding world

We need to teach our children the emotions of happiness and the activities that bring them. We should stress the primary emotions of happiness, and the value of honesty. We should teach them the importance of thinking positive and loving thoughts. And most importantly, we need to teach them to be actively engaged in doing worthwhile things.

For example, they can feel the satisfaction of a good job that came from their efforts; they can have those feelings pointed out to them: the peace of mind that comes with honesty or the joy of learning. We can further encourage them by acknowledging their efforts. Point out the satisfaction they felt when they put all of what they had into something. They can feel the harmony in the home on each good day. We can express our joy in happy times in family prayer or around the dinner table. We can teach them what is truly valuable and to hold those things in their hearts with great worth- like their family, neighbors, and the earth, the life upon it, our freedoms, and our potential.

Our children can learn the satisfaction that comes from applying their minds, the peace that comes when they appreciate a beautiful sunset, and the delight that comes from well-planned family activities. They can learn the joy that comes from a community effort to feed the poor, or the sense of accomplishment when finishing a challenging project. They can learn that these are the things that are the substance of happiness and success.

They can learn that being independent, capable, successful, and happy come from knowing who they are and being true to themselves, and not from impressing their friends. They can be reminded each day when they leave for school to remember who they are and how much they mean to us. They can be taught to respect others peace of mind and their reputations.

Section 4
Self-reflection and self-knowledge

<u>The truth of who we are bears out more prominently when we are under pressure</u>

With pressure, a tiny and unnoticed crack in a vase can be discovered. The pressure of life can give us the knowledge of our weaknesses that are sometimes unnoticed when life is easy. Life will show us through opposition, evidenced through discordant emotions, that our beliefs are not working for us and our skills are inadequate. Life will show us that we have selfish and self-serving beliefs that are disrespectful towards others. Life will show us our appetites that are out of control.

Unfortunately, as we peer into the looking glass, our pride doesn't like what is peering back at us. Our doubts, our fears, and our pride can turn a blind eye and withdraw instead of answering the true challenge. We may even bury our emotional discord in a new relationship, but the unlearned lessons from life will have inevitable consequences.

Emotional baggage

The pain we feel with a loss relationship should not be replaced by a new relationship, until we have resolved why things did not work out.

The guilt we feel with things that are unresolved haunt our alone time- making being alone more painful than it is a time of solace. But this alone time needs to be our friend, even if this friend needs to be painfully honest. The choice to face and more fully understand our emotional pains, from time to time when alone, humbles us. It is a practice that creates a more attractive soul, a practice that leaves one more prepared for new challenges.

After a traumatic event, divorce, or death of one dear to us, we need time to heal and understand before we enter a new relationship with its own dynamics, its own hurdles, and new challenges. Any relationship is hard enough to make great. We shouldn't bring unresolved baggage into someone else's life. When we do not take responsibility for our emotions others have to feel the weight and consequences of them. These trials and their accompanying emotions have their own timetable, and without giving them adequate time to be resolved, and when under stress they affect us and tug at our new relationships in abrasive ways.

We need a hiatus between serious relationships in which to ask ourselves some poignant questions. A good rule of thumb is about one month per year after one relationship ends before we start looking for another one. This is time to evaluate our lives and how we related to others with respect to our boundaries. What can I learn from my experience? What could I have done differently? Did I allow someone to tell me how to live? Or did I tell someone how to live? Could I have been less judgmental? Were my wants and appetites put before the well-being of others? Did I appreciate the choices others made that was admirable? Was I intimate; did I listen, and make eye contact? Did I show an interested in their day and in their well-being?

<u>Our modern world has limited our emotional toolbox</u>

On average, our sedentary world has shrunk the toolbox of positive experience and has limited the kinds of emotions that people can relate to. Our music is a good gage of our society in general. What sells the most is what people relate to. Today popular music is angry, desperate, and oversexed…with little, to no unique sound for each artist. There is very little artistic uniqueness, and deeply talented or skilled contemporary music. The amount of emotions expressed in today's music is few and the kinds of interest and topics are few as well.

Conclusion

Our lives are like our own personal garden. Each garden has its unique beauty and challenges for each soul. Our agency is the gardener. And in this garden, as in every other garden, things grow at a natural rate. We will be changing throughout our lives. But if we take no effort to take out the weeds, trim the bushes, and prune the fruit trees- we will have a garden that is ugly and unproductive. We are the ones who have to take personal responsibility to know what kind of garden we want and make it beautiful.

We can look at our past to find conflicting values. Those things that we do, or hold to, that keep our gardens from flowering and bearing fruit should be eliminated. We can pull out some bad habits and unfinished business that choke the vital nutrients that we need to thrive in life. We can have that Garden of Eden, one that we build deep inside ourselves. The flavor of its fruit is joy, contentment, peace satisfaction and delight. If it is continually kept weed free with rich soil, it flourishes inside us and becomes a source of power, direction, and inspiration.

Chapter 8- Emotional Skills
Intra-Congruous Abilities

Like a skilled dancer
Through discipline, a goal within sight…
Controlled and precise
The ballet of emotions, careful not to take flight
The joy, the rewards, a feeling so great…
that perfect pirouette
Mastered through practice and grace
A love for her plight

Section 1
Becoming emotionally responsible

Introduction: Emotional road signs of our humanity

Life provides the signs that point the way for our humanity. Tragically we question why the sign is there, or who put it there. We think it is not fair that the sign is there. Mostly we wish the warning signs would just go away. The warning signs are our difficult emotions, telling us when thing needs to be done.

In this world when we aimlessly travel, many times on hazard-filled paths, the warning signs of emotion tell us when to stop, use caution, turn back, construction in process, when to go, and when to go faster.

What if my body never ached when it was sick? Or what if my car didn't start to act up or make sounds before it became a total wreck? The warning signs and emotional pains disclose that something needs to be done before a crisis takes place. So many times they start out as quiet sounds and get louder as they are ignored or misdiagnosed. The earlier we can see the warning the better. They can, if we listen, tell us the smallest fine tuning that we need to make in a voyage to the most worthwhile destinations of personal success and contentment.

Emotional skills are used for all intra-personal struggles

Emotional skills are intra-congruous abilities we wisely use around our emotions, moods, imagination, attitudes, attractions, appetites, and desires. In other words they are cognitive abilities that direct our subjective processes of perception and motive. They direct these subjective forces to be in harmony with things as they really should be and can be. They are also called intra-personal skills. We will call them intra-congruous because we will stress their wisdom be aimed at the two paths congruent to who we are- "Our North-Star." See illustration 7, Ch.5 Section 2. We will create skills to proactively create emotional strengths and congruous activities.

We call skills that are used to understand and navigate our emotions, emotional skills. The skills are not from the wisdom of emotions themselves, any more than a sign can have wisdom; these skills are cognitive. They are tools used by our agency. Using cognition to bring us healthy behaviors or states of mind is true with any kind of intelligence- whether it is social, spiritual, or intellectual. Ultimately it is our subjective chaos that is causing our woes in different facets of our lives.

Our agency is the captain of the ship and takes responsibility for its course and the behavior of all its crew member. In this ship of the soul, even the subjective force of thought, one of the captain's crew, is controlled or neglected by it. We are accountable for all subjective activity. The captain's best answer is to choose the reasoning of respect and love to understand, control, and respond appropriately to our subjective world.

We need to take your emotional temperature often. Throughout the course of a day, pay attention to your moods, desires, and attitudes. Though our preconscious world is not so lucidly up to our agency's view, with constant vigilance of our emotional state, we can begin to be more aware of our inner world. Agency can use emotions as evidence of deeper more preconscious thought.

Each stage in life has its appropriate level of emotional skill

Our intra-personal skills need to grow in parallel to our age. Again we do not expect a three-year-old to handle adult relationships or sexual thoughts. By giving them too much too soon, we harm their sense of self-worth and make it more difficult to reach their potential. Building intra-congruous skills takes time, they are critical thinking skills, emotional skills, patience, creativity, and the habit of constructive imagination.

Words and pains reflecting emotional immaturity and irresponsibility

In our self-awareness, as an adult, we need to pay attention to selfish and prideful words that accompany negative emotions. Things I think or that I say, like, "I want…" "It's not fair." "I," "me," "but..." "If only 'you' were better at...," or "If only 'you' would stop doing this," should put up red flags in our minds. These are a sign we are unwilling to take responsibility for our own emotions and discordant attitudes and choices.

No emotion that I feel is proof someone else is at fault

We not only need cross our words but pay attention to habits, behaviors, and pains. All discordant emotions (other than loss) such as worry, sadness, and anger are signs we need to take more responsibility for our lives. Other sings of not taking enough responsibility are lower back pains, headaches, bad habits, stress, and anxiety.

Section 2
Beginnings of emotional intelligence

The first intra-congruous skill to master is an emotional skill called emotional awareness. It is to become more quickly aware of our clamoring feelings, so as to not react to them. It is to acknowledge the "road sign" when it is still at a distance and not after it has already become difficult to act with forethought and grace. We can be aware of our emotions as they begin to sprout.

We need a quick awareness of our emotions, moods, appetites, desires, and attitudes. After this quick awareness, we can take the next immediate step and that is to take ownership of the emotion- instead of our emotions taking control of us. Affirmations of awareness, for example, "Am I doing this because I am being manipulated by guilt?" "I am beginning to be angry." "I'll take a deep breath and ponder, 'why do I think I am better than someone?'" or, "I am beginning to lust..." I am beginning to objectify others", "I can redirect my interest in something more admirable." And, "Only psychopaths do what they think and feel." "I can use my imagination to think of good things." If I am judging someone, then I could tell myself. "We all have equal potential." "Had I lived their life I might have done the same thing." "I should not box all of a race/sex/religion as having any particular attribute."

Keeping our emotions at a whisper

Our moods, emotions, and appetites come and go. We need an awareness of our internal world to regain and keep our emotional balance before it becomes too difficult to catch. We need to keep our emotions at a quiet whisper. It is hard to be objective and humble enough to admit we are judging when the anger gets intense enough to fill our souls. But we can get in the habit of being more humble as we develop better awareness. We can catch anger, sadness, greed, lust, and prejudice before they are more difficult to manage.

Catching our emotions and tendencies early is the first step needed before taking emotional control. If we do not take control of our emotions when they are still at a whisper we will need even more of an emotional skill called forbearance. With this skill, we do not ignore or "react" to strong discordant feelings or strong self-destructive desires. We just tell ourselves, "It will be all right, I'll be OK," until our emotions get back to a whisper. We wait until our emotions are at a whisper before we think, say, or do something. Most of us simply "react" to emotions immediately. We act without respect, and without having a worthy purpose.

Affirmations- the key to creating emotional forbearance

Forbearance is not to dwell on the emotion and ugly thoughts which would normally intensify our emotions. Forbearance is to not panic over the emotion and it holds the emotion in check while we better prioritize. It is to take ownership of our emotion we have become painfully aware of. Forbearance uses affirmations like, "I am to blame for my feelings." "I'll relax, empty my mind, take a walk, and in just a bit I'll think more about why 'I' and feeling this." If I am busy and don't have to deal with this emotion now (we rarely have to deal with them immediately). "I'll count to 60, while I think loving thoughts, I'll let the emotion subside and I will tell myself, 'I'll make it a great day and deal with this later.'" Forbearance is anything keeping our strong emotions in check.

Emotional high-jacking is when we allow our emotions to get out of hand and make rational thinking more difficult; we did not use emotional awareness, emotional assuagement, or forbearance. When we blow small things out of proportion because emotionally we have made it a big deal. We rehearsed and ruminated over our woes too much. Moods and desires also highjack our rational mind and make self-control more arduous.

Strong discordant emotions overpower our empathy.
They steal from our hearts the equal worth
We hold for others.
Leaving us thoughtless, selfish, and proud.

In forbearance, we remind ourselves that the emotion is not something to fear and panic over but it is a friend warning me that I need a course correction. For example, we should not "react" to the emotions of being irritable, lustful, angry, jealous, self-pity, fear, or sorrow. If we ignore the emotion we tend to be thoughtless and unkind.

<u>Affirmations are great for creating emotional space</u>

First, there is an inertia to overcome. We are trying to create a "space" where I can see the physical effects of the emotion on my body, and its effects on my thinking, and let them dissipate to a whisper. The skill to perceive how emotions affect me physically is called Interceptive awareness. The "creating of this space" is called emotional assuagement, it is the ability to calm our emotional state leaving psychological space to think and ponder from.

Emotional assuagement uses affirmations like, "It's going to be OK." "I'm going to get through this," "they have feelings too," "maybe it is not as bad as it seems to be." Affirmations like these go a long way in keeping the emotion from overwhelming us as well as curb our tendency to punish others with our emotions. We are substituting negative thoughts for positive ones.

Affirmations are truisms we think of in advance, before our need to use them, because of our humble knowledge of our weaknesses. If we are prone to envy, we can tell ourselves, "I am happy for them." If we lust we can ask ourselves, "Is this what I want to be?" or "This only leads to sorrow." We can remind ourselves of the ugly consequence of uncontrolled appetites and their impact on everyone else.

Affirmations in creating our emotional boundary

Whenever we catch ourselves dwelling upon negative thoughts and abrasive emotions, we should not only see its ugly nature, but we should also think of the virtue we should have had that would have prevented this. Boundaries are built in the defense of virtue and of our humanity because of their worth built within us. Boundaries are virtues of entrustment. For example, If I lust for the neighbor's wife, I should not only see an angry husband and my own wife with a broken heart, but I can see this ugly desire as a road sign of needing to respect and honor my wife more and give her all that is truly hers. Can I imagine loving my spouse more creatively and effectively? We are not just trying to stop in our vice but we should be trying to replace it with the reciprocal virtue.

Affirmations bring hope and equal worth- using anger and sadness as examples

Anger and sadness are closer than you might think. They usually hold the same grievances of lost expectations except sadness tends to dwell on its hopelessness and anger focuses on arrogant judgments. Some might do both. Anger is frustration mixed with pride. It is judging itself better than others or judging a situation as unfair. But because of pride, instead of turning to pity or sadness, it turns to self-righteousness. There is no anger without pride.

With sadness, we need to find truthful affirmations building hope, and with anger, we need affirmations that build equal worth and potential. Like, "Had I'd been in their shoes I might have done the same thing." But with every discordant emotion, these two kinds of affirmation cover them all. 1) Affirmations that bring to mind hope, based on the motive of love, and 2) Affirmations that bring more sense of the worth of things, based on the motive of respect.

Affirmations of love and respect
Are the hub of change we all need,
They bring the peace and belonging we all yearn for.

Illistration 8: Emotional Skill - as easy as 1..2..3

<u>Emotional Resilience- our most useful emotional tool</u>

Emotional resilience is the ability to more quickly leave an emotion then steer to another emotion or preoccupation. It is also the ability to allow for the emotional pain of loss to be budgeted, to leave it and review and ponder its meaning for my humanity when the time is more appropriate. This particular skill is responsible for most of our coping in difficult times. We can leave and revisit the memory of our emotions with our own growing wisdom, according to a more purposeful agenda, to a more balanced life.

With emotional resilience, we can enjoy our lives and allow others that share our lives, the same courtesy.

Most of these skills happen in just moments as we try to catch our emotions, moods, and desires. We are quickly and creatively finding thoughts to curb them, assuage them, and create space for our better selves to take control. The more skilled we are in intra-congruous abilities the faster the process takes.

With the emotions of the loss of someone very dear to us, we will certainly feel again and again for quite some time. And, we should let them out from time to time. But with emotional resilience, we can keep at bay the feeling of loss when we are at work or while we tend to our children.

Worrying about our problems throughout the day, when there is nothing we can do about it, will adversely affect our judgment and health.

Section 3
Emotional discord and confusion

Discordant emotions are mostly for categorical convenience. They are not always painful. They should be in consideration in our lack of virtues, skills, and respect for certain criteria of our humanity. They are not about finding fault with other individuals or making conclusive judgments of ourselves like, "I am a horrible spouse." It is far more honest simply to observe our behavior and describe our choices, through the lens of respect and love for our humanity.

Illustration 9: Discordant emotions

	Pride, Fear, Doubt	
5 Unique sets of human potential	Emotional discord & other signs of incongruous paths from "who we are"	Answer to errant paths to human potential
1 Gaining knowledge	Diffident, Obstinent, Stupid Stubborn, Oppinionated	objectivity,humility faith, study skills
2 Gaining creativity	restless, depressed, anxious, worried overwhelmed, hopeless, dispair, sad bored	positive imagination E.Q. need worthy purpose
3 Gaining virtues/skills	incapable, humbled, frustrated, trapped	self-improvement work ethic
	guilt, shame, unworthy	held accountable
4 Gaining self-reliance	indifferent, complacent, envious	empathy
	envious, offended, self-pity	held accountable
5 Gaining unity	unloved, unwelcomed, lonely, disrespected	need worthy purpose find respectful & trustworthy freinds
	angry, contentious, irreverent, irritated impatient, jealous	humility, empathy patience

(In the illustration, the discordant emotions point to where we would be falling behind in the pathway towards "who we are." On the right are the pathways we need to take. We do not come to enjoy life because we stopped hating, we enjoy it because we started loving.)

Trying to "make" someone else feel bad
Never brings happiness or potential to anyone

Most of our emotional pain, our frustration, anger, sadness, envy, diffidence, jealousy, dissatisfaction, and chaos in life can be traced to these two things:

First: Lack of respect:

A) Not holding self and others to be of equal and infinite worth.

B) An unwillingness to honor the boundaries between us.

C) Allowing disunity and disharmony with self and others.

Second: A lack of love:

A) Not making appropriate choices for our gifts of humanity.

B) Not taking responsibility for finding joy in our gifts and with each other.

<u>Attributing discordant emotions to things unrelated to our humanity</u>

The problem we have is we misinterpret the meaning of our discordant emotions. We read the signs wrong. An example is the discordant emotion boredom and its harmonic answer admirable activity. Although the rightfully associate boredom with unhappiness, many wrongly associate pleasure as the answer to their boredom. They are unrelated. Boredom is the lack of appreciation of admirable things. We are doing things that are of value to our humanity.

<u>Complacency- a spiritual slumber, a false sense of security</u>

Another important discrimination is between complacent and content. Complacence is not the same as satisfied or content as with the natural outcome of work or life. Complacency has apathy mixed with it. Complacency is not so much as an emotion but a belief or attitude. It is a state of mind that simply is not miserable. It is a compromise forged by our lethargy and selfishness. It is saying this is good enough even though the job is half done or even when there will be consequences from our lack of character.

There is no stagnation of human character. Either we care about reaching our potential and it grows with the effort, or spiritually we die in complacency. In life, when something stops growing it dies.

Like, if we were to stop watering our gardens because we are complacent with them, they die. So it does with our humanity. The majority of the human race live reactionary lives. They hardly experience what their humanity is capable of. To them, complacency is happiness, not having the real thing to compare it with. But because it is without any depth of character, even their time in complacency is limited by their next breach in human boundary.

Section 4
Intra-congruous and interpersonal skills

Hereafter is a rough list of emotional skills as ideas where I might creatively build, where I need to build emotional dexterity. And though some may seem at odds with each other such as masking an emotion or letting it out, we decide what is appropriate in each particular case. After reading the list, think of one that you need more than the rest and ponder and work on it. The first four should be learned in order.

(Important exercise: Think of three affirmations apropos for each, and six for any you may personally have difficulty with)

<u>Intra-congruous skills</u>

1) Emotional awareness is the ability to quickly recognize my moods, emotional state, psychological or physical appetites, and their intensity before they escalate further and before I react to them.

2) Interceptive awareness is the ability to be perceptive of how my emotions and moods affect myself physically. The ability to be aware of how charged my voice (or body language) is with frustration, anger, concern or any other mood or feeling.

Some emotional baggage we just don't want to let go, such as deep resentment, self-pity, sadness, and anger over longer periods of time… can cause physical diseases, even cancer.

3) Emotional forbearance is the ability to feel an emotion or appetite without reacting to it. It is the ability to mask emotions when I need to.

4) Emotional assuagement is the ability to soothe myself when in distress and emotional pain. Here I begin creating space from my emotions to think more rationally. With unhealthy appetites, I can find something admirable to do instead that brings satisfaction to the soul.

5) Emotional resilience is the ability to tuck emotions away and revisit them at more opportune times.

6) Emotional creativity is the ability to create positive feelings by their avenues of related efforts, (esp. admiration, connected, joy, content, peace, satisfaction, appreciation, and peacefulness)- like savoring the satisfaction of doing a quality job, or doing a service project and caring for those less fortunate. Choosing to smile and be friendly. The ability to hold people with infinite value. The ability to hold things of deep worth and feel gratitude in the soul for things sacred or of real value.

7) Emotional channeling is the ability to let out my emotional pain in safe productive ways, as well as waiting to do so at an appropriate time (like a good cry from time to time). Take a walk, go out to the garage and hit a punching bag, watch a movie. Avoid punishing others by my emotions, or being too emotional when I talk to others, first, let them subside.

8) Delay of gratification is an ability to be patient in waiting for what I want, or waiting till appetite subsides. Hunger comes and goes as well as appetites. I can prepare for what I want, find other things to do as I wait. It is also the ability to relinquish my desires for temporary satisfaction for more substantial activities that promise more admirable rewards.

9) Pleasure borrowing is the ability to anticipate a favorable outcome. Imagine the ripple effect of the desired results. Who

benefits and how? How will they feel? How will I feel about it? In what ways will I benefit?

10) Emotional anamnesis is the ability to find the beliefs, events, or sources of my feelings and appetites from my previous experiences. When was the last time I felt this? When was the first time? What did it mean to me? Is it influencing what I am feeling now?

11) Emotional empowerment is the ability to motivate and energize myself to move towards and succeed in my goals. It is the ability to see the worth in learning, in practicing and in excellence. It is to motivate myself to try again. It is an ability to build confidence in truth, and in life.

12) A Large emotional toolbox is the ability to identify with many different kinds of feelings, allows me to have more understanding of myself and empathy for others.

13) Emotional dexterity is the quickness in which I can change my emotional state.

14) Emotional congruence is the ability to attach emotionally in proportion to those things that matter. I am not blowing up over small things or being indifferent while I am watching my toddler run out onto a busy highway.

<u>Inter-personal and group skills</u>

1) Interpersonal emotional perception is the ability to read the emotional state of others.

2) Emotional attunement is the ability to reciprocate the emotional state of others.

3) Emotional propriety is the ability to give proper body language, facial expressions, and eye contact.

4) Healthy emotional distance is the ability to create emotional distance in relation to the amount of time, trust and intimacy that has been reached with others. An ability to be hopeful in proportion to probability.

5) Empathetic and Emotional sophistication (with those close to me) is the ability to correctly perceive the intentions of others. The ability to see and accept what is real in those with whom I share my life and make decisions, based on what is real. Perhaps I just will not accept the fact someone will not return my love I give?

6) Emotional tolerance, when apropos, is the ability to choose to remain unresponsive to the emotional state of others.

7) Empathetic congruence is an ability to keep from gaining pleasure with other's failures and pains.

8) Emotional influence is the ability to motivate and help lift the moods of others.

Congruous group skills

1) Social attunement is the ability to entrain to the mood of a group or choose to abstain from the mentality of the group based on sound choice.

2) Emotional influence is the ability to motivate or calm a Group.

Section 5
Questioning emotions

Stopping emotional high-jacking, creating space and understanding

The high-jacking of appetites and emotions are cause for most of our regrets. With our daily emotions, moods, and appetites, we can ask ourselves questions that create emotional space and personal responsibility. Here "Space," means reaching and attaining a calmer emotional state so that we are able to think more rationally and take the blame for them. "Responsibility," means reminding ourselves that this emotion came from my beliefs and is about my humanity. What does it say about me? What does it say about how I relate to others?

Moods are a mild emotional hum that lingers. It is like carrying an attitude around with me. To the reactive personality these moods, like emotions, are contagious. (Emotional contagion).

Hereafter are questions that help keep us from faulting many of our moods or emotions to others. This intra-congruous imagination helps bring harmony in the lives we share with others. We ask ourselves questions such as these when our mood is low, "Perhaps my mood is low partly because I have just overworked myself?" "Perhaps I haven't slept well?" "Perhaps I haven't eaten healthily?" "Perhaps it's just a dark overcast day?" "Maybe I still am a little upset that I failed a test earlier in the day?" The possible questions are endless as our imagination.

It is the mark of great wisdom and personal self-control,
When we choose to question our emotions and desires
Instead of reacting to them.

Being aware of our moods, and emotions, and then questioning them, help to keep us from reacting to them. Questioning our moods gives us more emotional freedom than the answers do. With strong emotions, buried or not, the answers are extremely helpful to know the source of our feelings, but still not necessary. We may not know why we tripped but we still can learn to walk.

Section 6
Answering moods, appetites, and attractions With intra-congruous ability

<u>Our moods gravitate to four categories</u>

Introverted, prideful

1) Diffident: pessimistic, melancholy, inadequate
2) Unstable: irritable, rudderless, and reclusive

Extroverted, unpretentious

3) Confident: optimistic, happy, and empowered
4) Stable: content, pensive, gregarious

With our moods the more we are set in our desire to quickly find any one specific reason for them the harder it is to just leave them behind. Just give several probable reasons. The important thing, with moods and emotions, is not to get fixated on them. We needn't get depressed or panic over them. We need to quit worrying about how happy or sad we are, at any one moment in time, and focus on choices that bring the emotions of happiness to life.

When our moods are low, or when our emotions rob our peace of mind, a few loving affirmations now and then can help guide the chatter and appease our souls. It may take some repetition through practice and habit before we strongly believe all we affirm to ourselves. Their power increases from being continually instilled into our preconscious minds. Our affirmations should be questions that diffuse blaming people, even myself, these next questions are to comfort and give direction, putting hope in truth.

Congruous and positive questioning can help us get through until we are in a better state of mind. Affirmations for emotion can also be used for moods. "I can get through this." "Everything is going to be alright." "It's not their fault'. "I don't need to take it out on them." "It is important for me to get through this." Instead of, "I'm stuck," we can affirm that "It's a challenge to rise to."

Our emotions and moods point to thinking that we are probably unaware of, or in denial of. With 60 thousand thoughts per day, our emotions are a good summary of what they have been. Affirmations help us cope and be kind to ourselves and others, and slowly replace our internal chaos and negative chatter. With enough time and practice, these affirmations are more second nature and easily come to our conscious minds without much effort. They are small means with tremendous benefits to our pre-conscious mind. By accumulative influence, they build healthy boundaries and powerful forces within our soul.

<u>We are never stuck in one emotion such as depression</u>

For some people, getting out of constant depression has become a difficult challenge. One reason for this is the belief we can only feel one emotion at a time. We can feel more than one thing at one time. We can even feel drained and tired and still feel at peace, or satisfied. Another reason is that they believe in their doubt and the spiritual abuse of psychologist in today's world that like medicating.

The way out is constant proactive efforts, and proactive behaviors. The answer is to continually bring the emotions of happiness until they begin to have more effect in the minds habits and lingering chemistry than the depression is. The law of opposition says the deeper the depression and longer its therapy will be.

Building the boundaries that keep depression away

Depression can be treated as any broken boundary and boundaries can be hard to rebuild. They are "rebuilt" through the pairing of "both pathways" of imagination and constant effort (See Illustration 6: "Pairing of Entrustment and Hope" Ch. 4 Section 4.) Building creativity through art and the practice of seeing new options, emotional and critical thinking skills, empathy, service, and kindness. We have to build a strong affinity and admiration for those things that are virtuous and admirable.

We have incredible ability and creativity when it comes to our emotions. It just takes a few affirmations, questions, and some skills. Unlike thought, which we have one at a time, emotions linger and mix. We can ask when we are depressed, "What is there that I am still blessed with?" "Have I called and told a daughter I miss you and love you'? "Do I find a kind friend to have an eye to eye conversation with?" We need not fear, embellish, or be consumed by the mood. Nothing brings more joy than giving joy to others like, helping someone that is having a hard pregnancy, or an elderly person that can't keep up their yard. We choose to be happy regardless of the forces that vie to drag us down. Even with our moods tugging at us, we can still have empathy for others that come our way. We can feel good with them when they feel good, and we can have some joy together with those we comfort.

No mood, we feel for any length of time, means we are broken. There are no genetic precursors to inescapable sadness or even free happiness. We cannot mix the road sign with the road. Nor is there any emotions that linger that will cause us to be unable to cope. Our agency has the final say to who we will be (in any way). Even our personalities are not genetic certainties, with enough time and the right effort, we can be whatever we choose to be. A little imagination and creativity embrace the entire world of opportunities.

Desires, attractions, and sexual fixations

Strong sexual drives, desires, and attractions are cognitively contrived. They have been slowly and deeply carved into our preconscious minds. What, at the time may have been seemingly small and indiscriminate ingratiation may cause very ugly repercussions on our humanity. Appetites, attractions, and sexual fixations may be culturally accepted or frowned upon but they are not genetically determined! They can be changed by intra-congruous struggling and enduring practice. These abuses can be treated the same way the self-abuse of depression is treated by building new boundaries according to personal goals.

Humans are extremely resilient in what they can do and make of themselves. Our potential is so unfathomable that our limitations are measured by our ignorance. Anyone can purposely change their attractions, or base desires with the sufficient intra-congruent effort that is needed.

Section 7
Words to never confuse

Most of what bring us discordant emotions, especially those most parenthetical in our lives come from a false perception of the nature of those things most vital to who we are. We confuse terms that seem related. One such group of terms is feelings, thoughts, moods, desires, and beliefs.

The words think, feel, hope, expect, know, and believe should be flagged so that we can momentarily stop and reflect the accuracy of our beliefs and the direction of our feelings. To use these words without discrimination is to make it very difficult to take responsibility for them. Does this sentence really express how I feel or does it express a belief based on "facts?" How much probability is there that the judgment or belief might be true? Saying the word, "Feeling" doesn't make it a feeling. Saying the words, "I know," doesn't make it any more or less than an opinion. If I say, "I feel you will go," it doesn't change the fact that "you will go" is not a feeling. It is far better to say, "When I believe you will go I feel sad," or "When I think about you leaving, I feel unappreciated." Do we say, "I need," when it is really an unhealthy desire or appetite? Accurate statements leave less confusion and make for better decisions.

It is also vital to know the difference between affection, intimacy, love, sex, lust, appetites, wants and needs. Without the distinctions between these, we will make choices that bring heartbreak and leave us feeling unworthy, incapable, and unloved. Intimacy is most central to our happiness and has nothing to do with sexual attraction or desires. But when many feel empty or lonely they look for sexual connections and can't find why they are not satisfied.

True needs, understood and taken accountability for, lead us to real and lasting satisfaction. If we believe something is a need when it is in reality just an appetite, we will end up justifying our choices even when they are rude or disrespectful. Yet still, we will find ourselves unsatisfied after all is said and done.

We can mix up affection and intimacy and choose to be too affectionate with those we hardly know and still feel alone inside.

Intimacy is as it sounds, (into me see) to be seen or understood as a unique individual by another, usually with eye to eye conversation over a period of time. It is to have my beliefs, hopes, desires, attractions, things in my subjective world, understood through conversation with a trusted friend. Intimacy is our greatest psychological need and is increasingly more lacking in our modern world. Respectful intimacy leads us to be understood, to be accepted, to feel of worth, and to belong. Affection is of physical touch that is gentle and meant to show that we "care."

Romantic love is separate from sex. No relationship or activity that is disrespectful should be called any kind of love. If it is going to be a romantic love it should have both, a loving relationship, and include romantic activities. The Romance is the beginning of, and the path of, choices intended to get to know and come to admire someone. More specifically to come to believe, with great probability, that this person will be capable of an intimate and affectionate relationship- before we commit to a monogamous relationship and before we there is any sexual activity.

Section 3
The Beautiful Person

Intimacy, "In To Me See"

Much of what we do that we consider the right thing is because we defined it that way. The casuist can argue definitions and what is ethical, but when empathy is developed what is ethical becomes second nature. Seeing into the hearts, feeling with others and understanding their stories seems to show us and guide us to do the right thing. Humility and empathy build moral souls. Humility and empathy is the real stuff our humanity was meant to have. They make a house a home. They are the fountains of gratitude and belonging that make our lives profoundly worth living.

Chapter 9- Humility
Honesty with Self

In a dark mist a child I stay
A mind that wanders…running, jumping, imagining
For an escape is my play.
And in a tenebrous cloud I hide
A heart that wonders…unassertive, hesitant, uncertain
But outward a man that shows pride.

Section 1
An honesty with ourselves

Just as love cannot be a reality in our lives without respect, there is no empathy in our lives without humility. Trying to see the world without humility is like seeing it through muddy glasses. A skillful critical thinker would first build a humble habit of self-honesty, daily taking a few minutes to ponder such questions as, “What biases might I possess?” “How do I truly affect those around me by my choices?" Without this, I would view the world through a lens that is self-biased and shallow. It is counterproductive to work on empathy without learning how to humble oneself

Humility is:

A) Self-honest, an objective look at myself, an intra-congruous effort to understand and embrace my humanity. Humility sets time aside, about ten to fifteen minutes per day,

1) To gain insight from a daily and valuable effort to know the truth of one’s own story through reflection.

2) To compare my potential “who I am” to my choices.

3) To reflect how my choices affect myself and others.

B) The virtue from a tendency not to think about the self throughout my daily activities: such as constantly worrying about one's self-esteem, wants, appetites, appearance, one's way, what one is accustomed to, or expects. Antonym Pride and arrogance.

Humility is a key element in building boundaries, of knowing where I end and where you begin, where my rights end and where yours begin. I need to see and understand my emotions, thoughts, habits so as to see where my accountability lies, to parry me from false accusations, and to help me take responsibility for my life.

Humility’s criteria on “evaluating” my story are focused on the gifts of humanity to question my choices of love and respect: That is, 1) Gaining knowledge 2) Gaining creativity 3) Gaining character and admirable skills 4) Becoming self-reliance and remaining free and 5) Gaining unity and worthy purpose with others.

1) Are my words and choices honest? Have I been straight with others? Am I striving to be objective? Do I put my faith in true principles and do I have confidence in my worth?

2) Have I used my imagination in productive ways, have I gotten involved in projects and jobs that require my imagination? Have I creatively found answers that benefit everyone, or have I demanded my way?

3) Have I done what I needed to be a capable individual increasing in virtues and skills for work and relationships? Have I been a good example for others?

4) Do I value freedom and self-autonomy? Do I take care of my needs, live within my means, or do I depend on others? Do I value others freedoms, their time and respect their choices?

5) Do I have good relationships? Is their peace and harmony in my life with others? How do my choices affect others? Have I been of service to anyone?

Many times when I think I have gotten somewhere, in other words, "I am not humbling myself;" life has its way of showing me that I am still at the beginning. I am humbled by life.

The residence in the assisted living communities that I manage come to a point where they finally accept that they cannot do certain things anymore. They are humble as a child as they ask for help.

Life will often show us we are always far from arriving, or we have fallen far from where we once were. When we know that we have far to go, going the right direction has far more important than where I am at. Humility is focused on the direction of our path. Is it going towards our potential? It does not pretend to arrive anywhere.

"An unexamined life is not worth living".-Socrates.

To know that all of us have a lot of learning to do, faults to overcome and that all of us also have different strengths and gifts is the accurate mirror we should hold up to ourselves and the clear window we see others through. We don't get to the mirror near often enough. Most of us don't take the time to audit ourselves. How well am I honoring the boundaries that separate me from you? How much do I allow others to control my life?

A good question to ask are questions about how I affect my world. "Am I telling my wife and children what to do?" Do I give them reasons to feel loved and valued?" "Am I open about my intentions?" "Do I ever give compliments and validate others efforts, their love, or even their creativity?"

I need to see my part in the success and failures of my life. Even when we reflect upon our imperfections, if we cannot see how they affect others, no real depth of humility will ever be reached. This can't be stressed enough. Humility is the complete honesty of my story, my beliefs, intentions, and how my choices impact my world and those who live in it. An example of such an impression might be, "Is my depression or constant anxiety bringing me out of synchronicity with my children and causing my children to feel unloved?"

Pride keeps us from seeing that we are as human as anyone else. It keeps us from seeing that we forget, lose things, accidentally break things, and leave things behind. It definitely fails to see how much we need each other.

After refusing to come clean a daughter told her father, "Dad from now on I'll be honest." He responds, "You'll be honest when you confess the lies you have already told and not until then." Because of a lack of humility, she will not let go of her pride and be caught in a lie. She lies to herself when she says that she can be honest in the future even though she cannot be honest today.

Many have rationalized, and I have heard it all my life, "everyone lies." I reply that the honest are those that come back and confess, apologize kindly, and then reveal the truth. They became honest only when they saw the harm their lies caused, felt the pain they had caused others, and confessed their lie to anyone they told it to or who was affected by it.

Even without the pride that blinds us, honestly taking a hard look at ourselves, not an easy thing. No two virtues are more interconnected and dependent on each other than humility and empathy. Having empathetic people who share our life, who mimic our emotions and facial expressions allows us to have a better mirror to see inside ourselves through the lens of another's perceptions. Without decent, empathetic friends, and caregivers- it is harder to achieve a deep humility and a deep understanding of ourselves. Still, we need to take accountability for who we are, and it is possible if we make a sufficient effort to do so.

Section 2
Nature of humility

Though being frank with ourselves might be hard but it is worth every effort, for it builds inner confidence. Humility can easily speak openly and honestly about the self. Humility's relationship to facts can speak of shortcomings and accomplishments with ease. It takes pleasure in simple beauties and the joy of being alive.

Humility is very accepting of others in their imperfection. And though those who are humble forgive others and apologize with "empathetic concern for the other", the humble person rarely feels a need to forgive others or demand an apology for one's own benefit. Humility never held a grudge in the first place. These are the affirmations of the humble, "It is O.K." "There is no need to be ashamed, we are all human." "I have my own weaknesses as well." It is pride that feels it has its reasons to forgive others all the time. It is so much better than everyone else. Now Empathy may apologize or forgive, but it is for the other's benefit.

Humility is open enough to be accepting of others with their weakness because it first explored the weakness of self.

Each time we hear about blatant crime and we say that it is beyond anything we could ever do, we are not being humble.

<u>Humility a virtue of respect is needed in building boundaries</u>

When I understand that violence and crime are committed by ordinary people like me, I will make better choices. I should not allow seemingly innocent looking people that I hardly know, access into what should be my private and protected life. Understanding that I am not above ever making any kind of horrible act I am more likely to build more solid boundaries and keeps myself safe. I am less likely to engage in crossing other's boundaries that lead to more horrific behaviors.

<u>Keeping our childlike humility</u>

Children are naturally inquisitive. They get excited when they learn to ride a bike or tie their shoes on their own. They know their world is much bigger than they are, and they are eager to grow and discover. Amazingly, even when children are just playing pretend, they are ever so real and beautiful. They are genuinely being themselves. They haven't learned to be fake or holier than thou. They learn so quickly and absorb so much around them, not just because their minds are young, but because they have no preconceptions, prejudices, and ego to hide. They are humble.

For young children, there are endless questions and no judgments. Every mistake is quickly forgotten. Every unkind word is quickly forgiven. Their world is big enough for everyone to be a part of it. They dream of being fireman, astronauts, and doctors. Without pride or arrogance, they tell us of the great things they were able to do for they share their delight and satisfaction in expanding their gifts.

The child of yesterday is still a big part of who we are. Let them live, play, and find and enjoy everything anew. No expectations just a world to explore.

Humility has an attitude of discovery leading to an expanding rich world. Would children put themselves down if they were not harangued, ridiculed, or seen it played in their lives? A childlike view of the world is not biased, like discovering the beautiful terrain on a vacation in a faraway land, instead of expecting it to look a certain way. They are not disappointed with what they see. They are just taking it all in. Humility is the prime characteristic of those that are approachable and easy to love.

The four most common lies we tell ourselves
They lead to anger, self-pity, and disrespect

1) Someone else is to blame for how I feel.

2) I am unhappy because someone else did not live up to my expectations.

3) If I had lived the other person's life, I would have chosen differently.

4) I could never do that.

Section 3
Humble in good and bad times

How much of any virtue one has attained cannot be measured. The fact that we are inadequate at these three should be at the top of our minds.

In the fast track to our humility we should constantly tell ourselves:
"I can be more loving."
"I can be more empathetic."
"I can be more humble."

As adults, we should hunger for more of these. Of any of these, we should never pretend to know how much we have, pretend to have more than someone else, or think we are even close to having enough. Their attainment is not up for debate or comparison. The evidence of their lack is in the loneliness or the disharmony and chaos in our lives.

We must strive to be humble when life is good

Being humbled and being a humble person is not the same. To see our weakness at the moment of our trial is to be humbled, to feel shame or guilt. This is not a virtue but a reaction. To see our weakness when things are going well is to humble ourselves. This is the virtue and not an emotion, we do not feel humiliated. We need to learn to see things in new ways, develop purer motives, and better habits before life's next test. This is the time of real growth. Most of us are humbled by circumstance and then when things are less intense, and we are not embarrassed anymore, we revert back to old habits. But our growth happens when we practice humility against its nemesis- complacency. When we are simply eager, as an individual, to grow in our potential.

We tend to be loving when life is good and humble when life knocks us down, but the opposite is what we really need to do. We need love most when life is hard and humility most when life is good. To don our humility, when life is prosperous, is the most beautiful character trait we can have.

And it's not that my love is blind
It's that I see your heart so well.

Humility a life with meaning

We find our greatest joys are not only in the moment but are from a deep connection to things as they are, like a beautiful sunset and a beautiful person. For, happiness lies in the path to who we are. Intimacy with others and even a greater honesty with the self makes things real and meaningful. No success, no awards or accolades, no trophies or titles will bring happiness to the soul not stripped of pride and that is depleted of empathy for others.

Chapter 10- Empathy
Receiving the Story of Others

My little one cried, her pain was great
When her teardrops fell mine did too
I was caught off guard, I didn't know
She is so apart of me, her pain is mine
Now she sees my tears, and she smiles and says
"Daddy, it's OK, I'll kiss the pain away"

Section 1
Introduction

"Playful and curious, always interested in the moment to moment interaction, empathy has the soul of a poet, the heart of a child, and the wisdom of a seer.....I have come to believe that empathy, more than any other human faculty, is the key to loving relationships and the antidote to the loneliness, fear, anxiety, and despair that affect the lives of so many of us" Arthur P. Ciaramicoli in his book "The Power of Empathy."

Empathy is the crowning virtue in the gifts of our humanity. This unique virtue of our humanity is nature's way of bringing to our hearts what our minds may have missed. It naturally leads to ethical behavior. As we strive to respect and love others, empathy makes our motives all the purer. Humility and empathy build a natural boundaries of ethical behavior.

Without empathy, we still live in a perfunctory world. One that is insipid, and colorless. We would feel disconnected and unloved.

Everything in this book up to this point is a precursor for empathy. We can focus on love and give its definition. We can go through the mechanics of logic and principles. We can determine the criteria for what is true to our humanity. But, we may still never gain the emotional connection to actually care enough to do what we know is right. We will still be apathetic and possibly cruel. It may even be in a world where I am generous but not from kindness, but for popularity or to feel good about myself.

-Touching Lives-
I asked God if He were proud of my life
He showed me the souls I have lifted
And the smile on their faces
I felt the love and the gratitude in their hearts
And I knew

Empathy sees no skin color, party affiliation, speaks no language and has no agenda. It sees only into the hearts of others, by the spirit of connecting and understanding, where deep inside we are the same. We all desire to be loved and cherished, we all hurt when we are treated badly, and we all hope for happiness. Empathy is to connect to that common thread that binds us together. It discounts differences in wealth, age, nationality…etc. In what matters most, we are a family.

Every empathetic encounter has a hint of joy mix with the sharing of other emotions. In our deepest sorrows, the taste of human compassion and understanding is a comfort and a gift of hope.

Section 2
What is empathy?

Empathy is:

A) To temporarily reciprocate the emotional state of others in one on one interaction.

B) The ability to receive, understand and appropriately respond to the story of others in one on one interactions.

C) An essential element in uniting each other in healthy bonds of belonging and understanding, especially after we reached an age of maturity.

<u>Empathy is a deeply humble and eager acceptance of others' stories</u>

Though empathy has a simple definition it is not easy to obtain. It is our pride and selfishness that gets in the way. Most think they are being empathetic, in reality, most just give sympathy. Empathy is objective and humble and must have these qualities in an "abundance" before it really becomes a virtue of any power. If we haven't dealt honestly with our own emotions we will not be able to appropriately respond to and deal with others. When others share their emotions and we are hiding from ours we will turn a deaf ear or even curtly or rudely cut the other off.

We pursue the virtue of humility by brief honest self-reflection- setting aside a small part of the day. We pursue empathy by a desire to lose our own preoccupation through the rest of the day and strive to understand others in intimate conversations.

Empathy is a receptive virtue. One cannot experience empathy and try to change someone at the same time. Someone is trusting me with their story. They are hoping to be understood, not corrected. They are not hoping to be judged or preached to. They need my considerate ear.

Empathy is born of intimate connections, eye to eye, heart to heart. With empathy, I am not only willing, but I am also “eager” to be affected by the intimate encounter of another individual. My purpose is to receive and accept their story. It is to receive and accept them. Loving others is not about agreeing with them but accepting them. Empathy connects soul to soul in its unique way and takes away loneliness in what can only be described as magical.

<u>Humilities relationship with empathy</u>

From humility, like fresh water flowing from a melting glacier, comes genuine empathy.

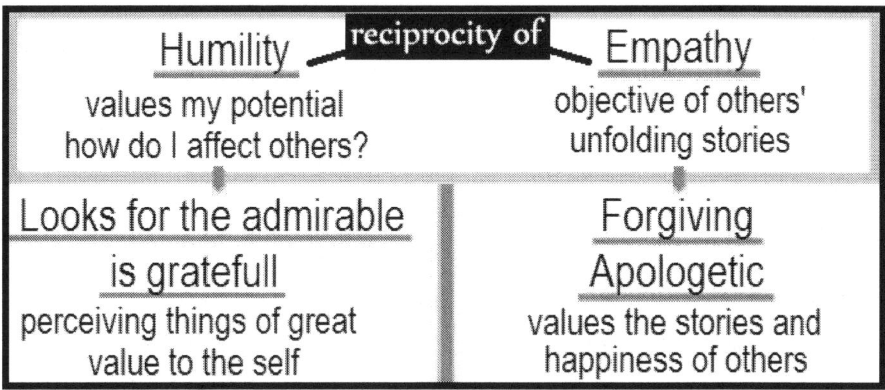

Empathy and humility come from the same source. They are made from the same thoughts, beliefs, and values. The humble voice inside us that speaks to self is also the voice that kindly speaks to others. The vigilance and emotional awareness toward understanding our subjective world is the toolbox for our understanding of others. The voice of humility inward is the voice of empathy outward; its tone, attitude, and visage. When we show empathy we do it humbly.

Empathy like humility is open, teachable, and impressionable. Just as humility listened, paid attention to, and looked to understand the self, empathy is open to others, to listen and understand.

With empathy, our tone is humbly and quietly just below theirs. It shows consideration for their pain and story. Empathy uses very few words. Most of the time, its only response is with a soft "ooh" (like that must hurt), or an "ouch" (as if I just got hit too), or a "Yay!" (As if I am excited too). These brief but poignant responses are more powerful than sermons. Showing others by our responses, and not our words, that we share their pain and joy. This shows understanding instead of simply saying we understand. It is a power the one who is understood feels.

Those rife with empathy and void of self-pity
Have hearts both pure and fearless.

<u>Empathy understands our sacred trust and is best paired with listening skills</u>

Those with empathy hold the story of others as sacred. They are trusting me with their reputation and their vulnerability. I will treat their story as if it were my own. Empathy brings reasons for gratitude and purpose in intimacy. Empathy's closeness, the bonds it creates, unites our souls and gives life meaningful depth.

Empathy's objectivity not only allows for new information but often gives its hints that it is eager to receive more. As I hear the story of another, empathy's affirmations to the self are, "Listen." "Forget my own story." "They don't need my advice, just my understanding." "Do not come to any conclusions." Empathy asks for more story, "What else happened to you?" "Why do you think you felt that way?" The patience of the listener seems endless, affirming to the one telling their story, "They have time for me." "I am important to them."

Emotions are the toolbox of empathy

The more feelings I can identify with, the better able I am to give empathy to others. They feel heard when I mirror their facial expression and emotion. Feelings are our toolbox of understanding and not our shared experience. No two experiences are the same for two different individuals. We may have felt differently about the same event but at one time in our lives we felt what they have felt: sorrow, depression, anger, fear, jealousy, trapped, hopeless, empty, lonely, joy, contentment, and so on. Telling our own story or being preoccupied with that story, instead of being engrossed in the story of the other, will disconnect the empathetic bond. The point is to try to mirror and pick up their feelings.

Try interrupting a teenager by saying "I had the same experience and so I understand your feelings." You'll find this unwelcome and resented.

With empathy we do not tell others what their feelings mean, we may ask them what they mean. When confused we could say, "Do you mean this?"…but the conclusion is theirs alone to interpret.

Section 3
The unique story of others

We may have had similar experiences that caused similar feelings in our past, but with empathy that is not "why," we are feeling their pain. If they felt something different about a similar experience, would we notice? Do we really have the power of empathy? People feel differently about the same kinds of events because they believe differently. Empathy is the power to understand their experiences from their point of view.

With empathy, there is no us against them, just a unique "I" and any one of the 7.5 billion other unique each of you that share my world. With empathy we don't see groups as having a collective pain, we see the pain of each individual.

Empathy is perhaps the most objective of all virtues. To truly be empathetic we must forget everything we think we know about someone and listen to their story with a new heart.

Objectivity, honesty, humility, and empathy are contiguous cars on a train. Like dominoes, objectivity leads to honesty, honesty leads us to be humble and being humble leads to empathy. This quartet of human virtues is the authentic internal beauty of who we are. They create pure motives.

Illustration 10: Domino effect of virtues

Virtues of Entrustment		
Motive of Respect →	**Objectivity →**	**Honesty →**
desire to hold our world, truth, and others as valuable	open to information, trust my physical senses	deepened sense of worth for the truth & speaking truthfully
→ Humility →	**Empathy →**	**Respectful**
compare myself to my potential, aware of how I affect others	open to others stories/emotions	strong character of respecting others

Just as empathy inspires us to understand, coming to an understanding leads to more empathy. Perhaps we were treated rudely by the bus driver. We would tend to judge the driver harshly. What if we heard that this person's friend passed away yesterday? With personal honesty, we understand that we too could have acted the same way had we been in their shoes. If we seek to understand the normal behavior of a two-year-old, like from reading a book on normal toddler behavior. With a little more understanding we might not be so harsh with them when they do obnoxious things to get our attention; they are just trying to feel connected to us.

Empathy comes from a fountain of pure objectivity. If we judge, bias, think we already know, then empathy is lost. If we are being empathetic we are looking for and caring about, what is unique about their unique story.

Each person's story is unique. When we judge others by a choice they made, we are judging them from a snapshot in time in the story of their life. Empathy is striving to understand each person's unfolding story. Empathy is not about taking a still picture, a single moment in time to judge. The story is the moving picture. We are not defined by a single action. We are all on different journeys, each journey is unique to each of us. Each of us has different upbringing and circumstances. We cannot know what we would have done had we lived someone else's life and it is arrogant to presume so.

<u>In making assumptions of others we are indiscriminately judging them</u>

Arrogance presumes to know the stories of the lives of others.
Arrogance presumes all in a group are the same way and believe the same way.
Arrogance presumes that I deserve my good station in life and others deserve their plight.
Arrogance presumes my struggles are the fault of others and that the struggles of others are their fault.
Arrogance does not see one's own mistakes just the mistakes of others. It is an ugly disconnect from one's own humanity.

<u>Imagination is an amazing tool for learning empathy</u>

In our world of memories, even the imaginary play we had as children made a difference in our total lives. Things we imagine become a part of us, almost as though we experienced them in real life. The times that we imagine things, like what would it be like to be in someone's shoes, help to build in us more empathy and wisdom.

Here are some typical questions for our imaginations to answer. To our preconscious minds the things we imagine become quite real to us. What would it be like to be blind before a beautiful sunset? Can you imagine this? What would it be like to be old and frail with no one to care for me? Can you imagine the loneliness the feeling of being unloved and having no purpose? What would it be like to be overweight in a society that worships skin and bones? Can you imagine being called names as an overweight child? Being passed over for many jobs? How would we act if we lost our child? Why do most marriages fail after their child dies? What kind of circumstances might have brought him or her to do this? Our growing empathetic compassion acts like our conscience. It teaches us what is appropriate and connects us as equals. This intra-congruous effort builds in us a tenderness for others' humanity.

Section 4
Being kind to myself

We still carry with us many events we have felt, seen, and done, as well as what we felt about them. Some irrational core beliefs may have been left unquestioned. We may still view events about our past, and have not questioned the judgments and sentiments about them that we made when we were younger, more unwise, self-centered, and ungrateful.

I hear many say they have no regrets about their past as if they are trying to avoid shame. Regrets are a normal part of life from which we all learn from. Is it possible someone never did a selfish act that hurt someone? No. Even if they forgave themselves shouldn't they still care about the pain and suffering they caused others? Those that can frankly forgive themselves, without apologizing sincerely and making restitution for their wrongs, are sure to repeat their offenses and treat others heartlessly. Regret is just saying this choice hurt someone and shouldn't have been made.

<u>The virtue of remembering our own pain</u>

Each emotion has its utility. Even regret, when kept at a whisper and in its proper perspective, keeps us humane- it maintains our empathy. Sometimes our regret maybe painful. All the more reason to welcome the remembering, our offenses were painful to someone else. I welcome the knowledge that keeps me humble and empathetic. I must accept and embrace all of me. I am not perfect, and I can accept and love who I am, regardless of what happened in the distant past. Who among us has not hurt someone? Without this honesty, I cannot have empathy for others who have regrets of their own.

We must keep in mind it isn't the challenge, or even our initial emotion to the challenge or trial, but the fear and anxiety over the emotion, and it is the self-pity about our plight that causes most of the hardest emotions to bear.

By not rethinking and embracing any significant events in our past, to a sufficient degree, we are struck by our spiritual growth. Somewhere in us a child still feels condemned, a teenager still fears not being accepted. By coming to understanding how we were fashioned, how each part of our lives leaves its mark on how we will act today, a deeper understanding of our story gives us a more sincere voice free from hypocrisy. Our hurt in the past can be a part of a shame we bury. Perhaps parents or caretakers didn't give us authentic affection. Maybe we are ashamed we were very needy for affection in the past; so now we are not affectionate with those close to us.

Our compassion should be extended to ourselves. Can we see the child or teenager in ourselves? Can we see him or her in our thoughts, and imagine holding him or her in our arms- giving the comfort and the words that heal. Instead of criticizing ourselves for our distant past, we can give ourselves a little empathy. We can tell ourselves, "I am a person of incredible worth." "This it is one of many behaviors I used to have, it is not who I am... and this is what I learned. I can tell myself these are the challenges of life that are answered and overcome by love."

Section 5
Making empathy more real

Think in probability and not final judgments, then extend trust from our wisdom

Everyone's story and emotions are theirs to share and make sense of. It is not our place to determine what the feelings of others should mean to them. Neither should we tell them how to feel. We may share in their story, but it is their story. For example, we shouldn't tell others they shouldn't be worried when they come to us in a panic. We can embrace them, and show them we care, through empathetic response. They need us to share in their pain. We can encourage them by saying, "I know you can get through this." But, the emotions that they feel are appropriate. Their emotions are their road signs to interpret. They are insights into themselves. The empathy that is given to them, will help them not to have to face their pain alone.

We need to let people feel what they feel and believe as they do. When we interfere with their story, whether by preaching to them, by telling them that this or that is what they really think or feel, or by telling them not to think or feel certain things- then we are interfering with their own consciences. The natural reaction for them is to protect their egos.

Even when they are angry at you, feel for them anyway. If they blame you, your best choice is to not let them push your buttons. Stick to a kind discussion on boundaries, not a discussion on their emotion. Feel for them but don't let them have the power to take away your peace of mind. Feeling for them means they are understood. It does not mean you agree with them, or that you must feel shame for their emotions. We are responsible for keeping boundaries. We are not responsible for others feelings.

With good empathy, we are helping someone more fully tell their story. We can show them we want to understand them, by saying such things as, "What else can you share that was important?" "When was the last time you felt this way?" "How did you deal with this'?" If they ask for advice, we can tell them our story, such as, "I felt...when... And I did this... I learned that..." The advice is what we learned from our story from our perspective. It is not what they should learn or do. Even if they ask what they should do, the honest response is, "I believe..., or my opinion is..." When some people give advice, though they give it as an opinion, they expect others to follow it.

By coming to feel "their" pain, they are understood and we are not traumatized by the experience. We are strong enough to help carry their load.

With empathy, we find joy with those who share our world

Putting our close family or friends wants before our own wants (not before our needs), is healthy and is a part of great relationships. And comes naturally with empathy. He says, "I'd rather go where you want to eat, my dear," and she says, "No love, I think we should go to your favorite place."

We think of empathy too narrowly as feeling for the pain of others, but feeling with the happiness of others is every bit as important as feeling with their pain. It also can't be avoided when we possess true empathy. When someone is sharing their story and they are excited, we feel excited with them. We cannot be bored with the topic someone is sharing and excited about if we have empathy. Feeling for that happiness of others is the ultimate touchstone of pure motive. We are in tune with others and ache with them and laugh with them.

Empathy thrives in an imperfect world but love is not complacent with it

Empathy's intentions are not focused on a guarantee that everything will turn out all right. Empathy's implied message is, "I'm not always OK and you're not always OK, but that is OK." But love's focus and the message is, "I'm not always OK and you're not always OK, but that is the challenge for the gifts of our humanity to answer and grow from." Empathy learns the story without bias or agenda, but the love in us wants to make a difference with their permission and hopefully with their help. The time it took to build a truly loving character brings a treasure trove of wisdom. Love and empathy is the pinnacle of positive influence.

Empathy's "intentions" are not about making a difference but its powerful presence does make a difference. Empathy is a very small means that brings about great results. In the voyage of our lives, when the whirlwinds come and the waves crash against the vessel, it is empathy that keeps us afloat and able to weather the storm. Its influence is healing, brings hope, and holds our relationships together. Many of those who have taken their lives might have had a different story if they had someone who had given them a lot of empathy. Those who survived the holocaust credit their survival to those close family bonds which they lived for.

-Love & Empathy-
You simply felt my pain when I was upset at you
You respected my opinion when we disagreed
You held me even when I was hard to be with
Your love holds us together and gives me hope

Section 6
Sympathy

For the purpose of understanding behavior and not having the right words to describe those behaviors, we will make a distinction between empathy and sympathy; because in our common language, which is culturally derived, they are interchanged as if having the same meaning.

For practical reasons, we will distinguish empathy and sympathy so that we have concepts that we can discuss and that reflect principles in our objective world. If in your mind you understand the difference between the two it will help in listening and appropriately reacting to each person's story. Truth is more than things as they are and as they were, it is also the possibilities of all that really can be. We need a vocabulary that brings out all our possibilities. We have separated them, words like intimacy, love, and sex to have their one definition. Understanding precludes responsible choice and purposeful living.

When people share their stories, listening and responding doesn't necessarily lead to an empathetic encounter. Our toolbox of emotions may reflect a less mature or more arrogant person. Empathy is the "ability" to understand and appropriately respond to the feelings and to the personal information that is given. Empathy is humble. All of us interact with others in discussions, but few in today's world interact with empathy. Instead, lacking humility and subsequent empathy, we react with pity and sympathy.

With sympathy, we do not have to feel with others, or even understand them. Our pride and arrogance keep us from being equal partners, like trying to mix oil with water. When we lack empathy we may tell them they shouldn't feel that way, give them advice, or critique their story. We are superficially reacting to them, more from our impatience or somewhat apathetic torpor. A part of us keeps a distance as if the other is diseased. Sympathy is more long-winded and slightly condescending. Even the words that sympathy uses to create a barrier.

Sympathy is somewhat sarcastic. Its overtone is, "What a mess you got yourself into." While our words say, "Poor you, I'm sorry you got yourself into this mess. All the pain "you" must be going through." With sympathy it's a pain we rather not feel ourselves, so we say as much as we can, as quick as we can.

It is probable that the sympathetic person doesn’t deal well with their own emotions and much less with others. In general, most of us overreact when feeling emotional pain- it is like pressing on a sore wound when we feel the pains of others. Some even get angry when you tell them your pains, even if they constantly tell you about theirs.

Our pride can give an illusion we care, even though we look askance at others pain, so we can sympathetically pat ourselves on the back and go on their own merry way. With empathy, it is a joy to share in others happiness. It is an honor to help carry their sorrows. It brings us to be patient with their story, for we are willing, and even eager to hear it.

Just as a young child doesn't understand and respond to sarcasm, because they haven't learned it yet, those adults who have no empathy do not respond well to it. With a lack of empathy, they have developed unhealthy ways of dealing with their own emotions and needs. Lacking an understanding of the real things they seek for kind of a fool’s gold. They either seek or indulge in pity.

The pity seeker

These people take little responsibility for their happiness and their part in caring relationships. Some were overindulged as children and were not held accountable for their responsibilities nor their emotions. Parents gave them a lot of pity. This is often the only facsimile of love they knew. Not all pity-seekers advertise their woes through sorrow, many do so through their anger.

The pity seeker treats pity in the way some treat food. It is used as a substitute for love. Sadly they only feel loved when they get pity. The feeling of being sad has been rewarded with sympathy, and sadness has become their preferred emotion. They just can’t get enough pity. They wonder why nobody has the needed energy and time to be wrapped up in their obsession. When we try to be empathetic with their plight, the sympathy junky may see this as a sign we don't care... we must not be listening. The pity seeker often seeks the sympathy of complete strangers.

The pity seeker does not want you to feel sorry with them, but to feel sorry for them.

They are not looking for you to feel their anger but expecting you to validate and justify it. They want to hold onto their reasons for their fool's gold.

They are not looking to be understood but agreed with.

They are constantly fearing, judging, finding blame, and seeing the worst. The more reasons for the misery the more reasons to be pitied.

Their sorrow and anger are proofs they are victims and weapons that they are right. Disagreeing with them leaves a foul taste in their spirit of self-pity.

<u>The pity indulger</u>

Pity is a vice derived from pride or self-righteousness. They want to pity themselves to have a sense of righteousness. They are better than others (they believe they are a more tender and pure human being than others) and their emotional pain proves that. Those that feed on this self-deception lack authentic humility. Instead of comparing their choices or story with their potential (humility), they are comparing their story to others lives (pride). They do not see that other's lives are just as full of trials as their own. They are fixated on "fairness" and they believe they deserve better and more. They are innocent victims of an unfair world. They believe they entitled to their fair share (in stark contrast to feeling entrusted with the things of great worth for which they have).

The blame falls from their lips from the slightest perceived inconvenience. They spend much of their thoughts on manipulations and making things fair. Empathy is less wordy than sympathy and it doesn't take sides. This is difficult for the pity indulger to accept. Someone feeling their pains doesn't sooth them, but someone hating their offender, or perceived offender gives them a sense of self-righteousness and validated pity.

Dealing with the pity seekers and pity indulgers

Though they do not respond well to empathy we should still have empathy for them and show it. Empathy is still the balm that cures. It just takes longer for the pity indulger. It is far better than to validate or possibly enable their distortion. We cannot even be 100% sure that all they want is to be pitied.

Truly listening like love is physically taxing. It takes energy to listen. Their need for sucking up all the energy and attention can be exhausting. We should give empathy and listen to their story until it starts to repeat. But, taking sides with them validates their negativity, or negates any solutions they may entertain. When we do not validate their blaming of others we leave open to them their possible compunction. When they discover their own part of the problem it makes taking responsibility a step closer.

We may respond, "You seem very upset. I hope the two of you can work it out." As always, empathy says little and lets them figure their story out for themselves. We can ask questions, which imply no advice or make judgments; questions that steer their thoughts in more constructive ways, "If you have any ideas that might help or solutions, I would love to hear them." If you are the listener, and you are the one that they are blaming, then talk about the boundaries that are disrespected without judgments or name calling.

Living with those who are constantly negative can be a challenge. Never judge, or tell them they are wrong… but you could say, "This is how I get through some hard times."

Section 7
The bonds of Love, gratitude, and empathy

As I sat in the living room I could hear my five-year-old son. As he ran to the door he was crying, "Mommy!" He had scraped his knee, and the feelings overwhelmed me. I felt his pain. There was a bond there. It was as if he were a huge a part of me, intertwined in my soul; I was surprised. I ached that I wasn't instantly there to embrace him in his need for comfort and connection to the one he loved. It felt like time slowed down like a dream that held me motionless. I felt inadequate for the responsibility of such a beautiful soul. There wasn't anything that could be said that could compare with being there for him.

-Shows in Your Face-
In your eyes, I feel all I could hope to hear
The smile you give me when I come home
Your Contentment that glows when I stay near
What is within your soul shows in your face
Your love I feel words could never replace

Humility wonders if we are truly connected and understanding. It seeks to understand more because it assumes we don't know everything, and perhaps even less than we think. It wonders, am I being understanding and compassionate enough? This is a part of the "want to love more" that brings so much more of what brings happiness to our lives. They want to love more that brings us deeper into the paths of respectful entrustment and loving hope. Are we really completely there for them when they need our comfort?

<u>Apologies and forgiveness are acts of my humility and empathy, each time we do so our character is strengthened</u>

The mixing of our worlds is a difficult challenge at times. All of us make mistakes and live far below the mark of those things we know to be true. All of us should be pretty good at apologies. We have had plenty of reasons to practice. An apology is an exercise in humility and empathy. It helps to break the cycles of pride, of being compelled to be humble, and complacency. It puts us into the practice of humbling ourselves and building the virtues that are capable of better relationships.

Apologies and forgiveness are best served with empathetic compassion and kind generosity

The virtues of respect are 'to receive,' as of worth, our world and others. It is a meaningful and personal experience; but kindness is: "our hope and efforts 'to show' in a tangible way someone is of great worth." It is as meaningful only its purpose is achieved through interactive experience. Kindness is a tool in the coterie of loving motive. It is a great partner to put with empathy. We receive others as valuable, and we treat others as valuable as well.

Both forgiveness and apologies are great acts of kindness driven from empathetic compassion. Paired with loving wisdom, we do these for others to show them they are loved and valued. But we also need to do these for ourselves, to constantly humble ourselves, and to more fully overcome our disrespect (by an apology) and pride (by forgiveness). People are unlikely to forgive when they believe they could have never done such a thing. Or they believe they're holding a grudge is getting wanted revenge on their offender.

An apology is aimed at the descriptive truth of the behavior, and the boundaries it crossed. It is not an effort to rid myself of guilt. Apologies should never be self-debasing, like, "I'm an idiot for doing such a thing." Instead, they should be descriptive, such as "I'm sorry I took and sold your guitar, this was a heartless thing to do. I'm sure it must have hurt you. You must feel betrayed. I will replace it and respect your things from now on." We are apologizing for our disrespect. We have not been considerate of someone's right to own their things. We explained it lacked love and showing we care for their feelings and rights. We are also explaining that we understand its consequences. And the apology included a promise of respecting property from then on.

Guilt is an emotion that says, "Stop doing that." Because I said I'm sorry doesn't also mean, I am a changed person. After efforts are made to understand, and time has passed in creating and congealing new habits of respect into my soul...and when I know the probability of that happening again is very slim, then I can let go of the residue of guilt I feel. No emotions are ever something to fear. If on occasion, after the behavior has long past been dealt with and overcome, and I feel some guilt when remembrance is pricked- then I can think, "This is good, this helps me to remember that my mistakes will cause others pain, and helps me to be more empathetic." Regardless of how slim I think the chances are that the behavior will be repeated, I still keep myself and others safe by not repeating behaviors that lead to it.

Apologies are not aimed for the forgiveness of those you harmed. It is more an act of promise, even a vow to be kind in the future and restore trust through time. We should not apologize and then ask for their forgiveness... just apologize kindly. It is not manipulation for someone's forgiveness nor should it come with expectations on others. They may not have the character to ever forgive, but that is not a reflection of how horrible you are. Sincere apologies are acts of kindness and consideration to others, and they allow you to humble yourself begin making a personal effort to change. Apologies help to turn course and sail to more favorable destinations. You do not need anyone's permission or their belief in you to do so. Sincerely apologize and begin to move forward.

The gratitude that comes from humility and empathy

We yearn to be understood, appreciated and loved. Empathy has the power to do these. Humility and empathy are the fountains of gratitude and belonging. We are part of a family, a neighborhood, a community, a nation, and a planet.

Sinew and blood are a thin veil of lace
What you are my friend shows in your face
-anon.

We are grateful for the experiences of others. As we sail through life we learn and gain strength from the odysseys that others experience and that they share. We have added wisdom and gain strength from the stories of others as though they were our own.

Gratitude is feeling and it is also a choice. It is a choice uplifts both the giver and receiver. It is a choice that brings people closer together. It is a message of love that is more substantive for someone is giving an example of why one thinks highly of another. Next time instead of saying, "I love you," think of a way to say, "Thank you for…." Speak our love through gratitude as much as we can in any other way. Give details and why you are grateful.

We need to ask ourselves. Are the only bonds, which our teenagers make, with their friends? Are we not reading to our toddlers, talking to, and playing with them? Are we taking the whole family on vacations? Children will follow the crowd far more readily when they have no deep bonds with their parents.

<u>Building the community and world that we want starts in the home</u>

Being there for them in daily concerns and daily activities is the glue that helps them get through the hardest times and stay true to what they have been taught.

<u>It is how we say and do it</u>

If we are not asking politely, then we are not asking.
If "I love you" isn't said sincerely, then no love was expressed.
If we apologized without humility and kindness, then we are not sorry.
If we forgive and hold a grudge, then we haven't forgiven.
Being honest and real is more than words.

Are we having meals at a particular time so that the children can be present, asking about their day? Do we talk to them for a few minutes at the dinner table, or before they retire for the evening- concerning their day, their feelings, and their challenges? Do we say prayers with them and for them in family prayers? Are we telling them how important they are? Do we tell them how much we believe in their abilities to work hard and accomplish anything they dream of? Do we limit their time in front of the TV, behind computer monitors, or phone screens? Do we get them involved in being with people who give service in admirable activities?

Conclusion

Though we live in a world with numerous concerns, the greatest waste in this world is not the depletion of the ozone or the erosion of the rainforest. Nor is it the burning of fossil fuels to their exhaustion. The greatest waste in this world is that we as human beings are so far from our potential. We stopped finding joy in learning, solving our problems, and accomplishing our goals.

The path toward ending war and hunger, creating successful families and successful enterprises… that path that brings needed inventions for clean and cheap energy, falling crime rates, and greater amity between nations- is simply a byproduct of approximating human potential. The answer to our world's problems is found in who we are, the culmination of those genetic allowances that bring human accomplishment.

Rising to the challenges of the day

We may think we are wasting our day and our time, but every day the sun rises the day is asking us to rise with it. We can only waste our own unrealized potential. When we do not rise to the challenges of the day, we fall behind and we become unready to be parents, providers, and true friends to the ones we love. But when the challenge of the day comes before us, if we continually answer by exercising our faith in truth, we expand our virtues, our character, and build a more beautiful and joyful world.

Dr. Victor Frankl, in his book A Man's Search for Happiness, "...it did not matter what we expected from life, but what life expected from us... Life ultimately means taking the responsibility to find the right answer to its problems and to fulfill the task which it consistently sets for each individual." Finding the answers to life's problems should be a practice in which each individual improves.

Life will show us that the lies we believe in don't work for us. And whether it's the cure of disease, a need for better energy, or a hunger for more beautiful relationships, life will always encourage us to meet our challenges, to quicken our pace, to stand a little taller, and then raise the bar. Life will challenge us to be ready for each stage it offers. Life will show us the beauties of excellence, and the pains of indifference. How will we answer?

Appendix

37202928R00109

Made in the USA
Middletown, DE
23 February 2019